The Song of Awakening

*A Guide to Liberation
Through Marananussati
'Mindfulness of Death'*

The Song of Awakening

*A Guide to Liberation
Through Marananussati
'Mindfulness of Death'*

Namgyal Rinpoche

Edited by Karma Chime Wongmo

BODHI PUBLISHING CANADA

The Song of Awakening,
A Guide to Liberation Through
Marananussati 'Mindfulness of Death'
Namgyal Rinpoche
Edited by Karma Chime Wongmo
First Edition: The Open Path, Boise Idaho, USA, 1979
Second Edition: Bodhi Publishing, 2022

BODHI PUBLISHING
705-333 Hedonics Rd.
Peterborough ON K9J 7R6
www.bodhipublishing.org
bodhipublishing@gmail.com

Cover: Jean Vartan and Olivier Lasser
Text Design: Karma Chime Wongmo and Denise Truax

Copyright © 2022 Bodhi Publishing [1979]
All rights reserved.
No part of this book may be reproduced in any form or by any means, electronic or mechanical, including photography, recording, or by any information storage and retrieval system or technology now known or later developed, without permission in writing from the publisher.

Canadian Cataloguing in Publication Data
Title: The song of awakening : a guide to liberation through marananussati 'mindfulness of death' /
    Namgyal Rinpoche ; edited by Karma Chime.
Names: Rinpoche, Namgyal. author. | Wongmo, Karma Chime, editor.
Description: Second edition. | Includes bibliographical references.
Identifiers: Canadiana (print) 20200269046 | Canadiana (ebook) 20200269119 | ISBN 9781895316391 (softcover) |
ISBN 9781895316384 (PDF)
Subjects: LCSH: Death—Religious aspects—Buddhism—Meditations. | LCSH: Meditation—Buddhism. | LCSH: Buddhism—Doctrines.
Classification: LCC BQ4487 .R56 2020 | DDC 294.3/443—dc23

Of all footprints
That of the elephant is supreme.
Of all mindfulness meditations
That on death is supreme.
                                           Buddha

Acknowledgments

On behalf of Bodhi Publishing, I would like to acknowledge and thank those who, at various stages, kindly volunteered to help prepare the publication of this second edition of *The Song of Awakening*: Bruce Cowen for scanning the first edition's text; Doug Smith, Catherine Scrivens, Deborah Pearson, Trudy Gold, Kirsteen McLeod and Judith Dremin for proof reading early drafts of the second edition; and Andrea Cowen for exploring possible images for its cover.

I would also like to acknowledge my gratitude to the following: the late Edie Meyers who drew the rose and dorjes for the interior of the first edition, which are now included in the second edition; the late Jean Vartan who provided the design and initial image for the second edition's cover; as well as thank Olivier Lasser who, more recently, skillfully adapted Jean's image for the final cover.

In addition, I would like to thank Denise Truax for her generosity, care and attention in preparing this second edition for printing, as well as Alain Mayotte, her indispensable aide, for providing her with technical assistance. I would also like to express my deep gratitude to Susan and Jeff Riches for their invaluable support and dedicated effort on behalf of Bodhi Publishing.

Contents

Acknowledgments vi
Contents vii
Venerable Namgyal Rinpoche – 1931-2003 ix
Preface to the Second Edition xi
Introduction xiii
The Setting 1
1. Marananussati 'Mindfulness of Death' 3
2. Concentration Is Present 9
3. Siddhartha, A Symbol of Every Man 11
4. Three Characteristics of Existence 13
5. Wisdom and Compassion 15
6. Symbols at Death 19
7. The Only Refuge Is Freedom 20
8. Choiceful Awareness 22
9. Awakening Consciousness Is Present 24
10. Awaken the Clarity 27
11. Dreams and Visions 28
12. Technique 30
13 The Practice of Mahamudra 31

14 Working with Question 33
15. Four Levels of Understanding Dharma 35
16. Putting Down Verbalization 36
17. Meditation Posture 41
18. Discipline—A Path to Union 43
19. Working with Hindrances 48
20. Right Effort 51
21. Flesh and Bones 53
22. Telepathy 55
23. Making the Ideal Real 56
24. Awareness Is Knowing, Is Mahamudra 58
25. Self-awareness, God-awareness 61
26. Regular Practice and Respect for the Daily Life 64
27. Five Similes of Mahamudra 68
28. Symbolism 73
29. *Anicca, Dukkha, Anatta* 75
30. The Only Work You Have 76
31. Through the Senses—The Transcendental 77
32. Fantasy 81
33. Resting on Fact 84
Glossary 90
Publications of Namgyal Rinpoche's Discourses 98

Venerable Namgyal Rinpoche
—1931-2003

A highly gifted teacher, influential in bringing Tibetan Buddhism to the West, the Venerable Namgyal Rinpoche (Leslie George Dawson) was born in Toronto, Canada in 1931 to parents of Irish-Scottish descent. In his late teens he attended a Christian seminary in Toronto followed by further studies in philosophy and psychology at the University of Michigan. He then became involved in the socialist youth movement in Canada, culminating in a visit to Russia to address a youth conference in Moscow in 1956.

Directly after, he travelled to England where he explored both the Western Mysteries and the teaching of the Buddha and began practicing meditation. While there he met his first teacher, the Burmese Mahathera, the Venerable Sayadaw U Thila Wunta, and soon joined him in Bodh Gaya, India, where Sayadaw gave him the novice ordination and the name Ananda. Following Sayadaw to Rangoon, Burma, on Dec. 21, 1958 at the Shwedagon, he was given the higher ordination and the name Bhikkhu Ananda Bodhi. After intensive meditation and studies in Burma, Thailand and Sri Lanka, he received the title 'Teacher of Tranquillity and Insight Meditation'.

At the invitation of the English Sangha Trust, the Venerable Ananda Bodhi returned to England in 1961 to be their Resident Teacher. That same year he was a special guest speaker at the Fifth International Congress of Psychotherapists in London where he met Julian Huxley, Anna Freud and R.D. Laing, among other notable figures. He spent the next several years giving extensive teaching in England and also established a retreat centre there as well as in Scotland. He returned to Canada in 1964 for a short visit and gave classes in Toronto. He returned again in 1965 and began teaching there on a regular basis and subsequently formed the Dharma Centre of Canada in Toronto in 1966. Soon after, a 400-acre property was purchased near Kinmount, Ontario, for the purpose of study-meditation retreats (and held in a Trust until 1972, when the Dharma Centre of Canada became a Charitable Corporation).

In the next five years the Bhikkhu (as he was called by his students then) taught mostly in Toronto and at the Kinmount retreat centre. During this time, he also travelled widely and taught in North America and abroad, accompanied by many of his students. While visiting Tibetan monasteries in India and Sikkim in 1968, he met the heads of the major Schools of Tibetan Buddhism: His Holiness the Dalai Lama, H.H. the 16th Gyalwa Karmapa, H.H. Sakya Trizen and H.H. Dudjom Rinpoche, as well as many other masters of Tibetan Buddhism.

After their very first meeting in Rumteck monastery, the Venerable Ananda Bodhi said that H.H. the 16th Gyalwa Karmapa had greeted him like an old friend and seated him beside him on the same level. On a return visit in 1969, he received full ordination in the Kagyu Lineage and the name Karma Tenzin Dorje Namgyal Rinpoche. In the Spring of 1971, in Green River, Ontario, on instructions from H.H. the 16th Karmapa, the Venerable Karma Thinley Rinpoche formally enthroned Venerable Namgyal Rinpoche.

On one of his visits to H.H. the 16th Gyalwa Karmapa and to H.H. Sakya Trizen, the Venerable Namgyal Rinpoche invited each of them to visit the Dharma Centre of Canada, resulting in their first historic visits to the West in 1974. Several years later, Khen Rinpoche of the Nyingma School, recognized Namgyal Rinpoche as an emanation of White Manjusri, the embodiment of altruistic, compassionate wisdom.

Until his passing, Namgyal Rinpoche continued to travel throughout the world giving teaching at centres established by his students in North America, Great Britain, Europe, Japan, New Zealand and Australia. His dedication to the liberation of all that live, along with his interest in all formations, was as tireless as it was vast. A master of Mahamudra, he was unique in his ability to encompass and bridge traditional and contemporary paths of liberation from suffering and the causes of suffering while transmitting the path of enlightenment in universal terms for the benefit of all beings and the world.

Preface to the Second Edition

More than four decades have passed since *The Song of Awakening, A Guide to Liberation Through* Marananussati *'Mindfulness of Death'* was first published, and over three decades since it has been out of print. Considering the continuing interest in the book and the importance of its subject, Bodhi Publishing welcomes the opportunity to publish a second edition of the remarkable discourses given by the Venerable Namgyal Rinpoche, so that they may be available once again for the benefit of all beings.

The only changes in this second edition consist of an updated biography of Namgyal Rinpoche, a new *Preface*, an added *Introduction*, a revision of *The Setting*, and an enlarged, amended *Glossary*. Aside from a few small edits for clarification, Rinpoche's discourses remain the same.

As in the first edition, they contain his pith instructions on the ancient practice of Mindfulness of Death, the practice of meditation in general and the classical practice of Mahamudra, the supreme path of enlightenment beyond concept, imagination and projection. They also include key teachings and references to all schools of Buddha-Dharma, Judeo-Christianity and the Western Mysteries, as well as modern psychology and philosophy; all disciplines in which he was a master. His transmission, simply and deftly woven throughout the discourses, retains and reveals the essence of each of them, which Rinpoche placed in a context relevant for this age.

The layout and design of the text, as before, were influenced and determined by the content, giving rise to lists referring to specific and general stages of meditation; prose, which often emerged as dynamic poetry bringing to light the essence, complexity and depth of the teaching; and koans or phrases traditionally created by the teacher to awaken in the student an intuitive "beyond words" realization.

Similarly, some points Rinpoche put forward briefly that may seem esoteric or disconnected from the context in which they appear, have been left in for the benefit of those to whom they will have significance, now or in the future.

Whatever errors or omissions this book contains is the responsibility of the editor; may they be forgiven. Whatever merit is gained, may it eliminate the seeds of strife and gladden the hearts and minds of all beings and bring them to complete liberation.

Karma Chime Wongmo

Introduction

The occasion for the following discourses given by Namgyal Rinpoche during a three-week retreat in August 1976, was precipitated a month earlier in Oslo, Norway. Approximately one hundred students from several countries had gathered there to receive teaching from him for an intended three-month itinerant period while living in tents away from commercial campsites. Although several subjects were proposed, ultimately, they all concerned the study, contemplation and practice of Buddha-Dharma, the universal laws and path of liberation.

Beginning in Oslo, Rinpoche gave discourses at each campsite, as well as spontaneous teaching along the way, as our caravan of rental cars travelled northward up the western coast of Norway. A few weeks later, after crossing the Arctic Circle, a country house near the hamlet of Storjaard was found for him, with an adjoining farmer's field where we could camp for some time before moving on again. Discourses[1], contemplative explorations and meditation continued in earnest. However, it soon became obvious that Rinpoche's recent teaching in other countries, especially the extensive travel involved, had taken a toll on his health and that he needed a period of rest and relaxation in a warmer climate. As a group we decided to release him from his

---

[1] In 2008 Bodhi Publishing published these discourses in *Right Livelihood and Other Foundations of the Teaching*. See Publications of Namgyal Rinpoche's Discourses' page for further information.

commitment to continue teaching until he had fully recovered. Accepting our consensus, Rinpoche decided to travel to the sunny island of Crete. He invited six students to travel with him, myself included. Once there, two more students that he had also invited joined us for a total of eight.

Upon arriving in Crete, our first priority was to find a suitable dwelling for Rinpoche and the two students who were attending him. Although this took time, it gave Rinpoche the opportunity to rest and relax at a small hotel on a beach along the Mediterranean Sea. After much searching, a modest villa was found on a hill by the coast overlooking the town of Khania.

Once Rinpoche's needs were taken care of he asked what we now planned on doing. Seeing that the warm climate and a few weeks of rest had begun to restore his health, we expressed the aspiration to do a meditation retreat under his guidance, if possible. He readily agreed and, perhaps considering his recent ill health, the meditation he chose for us to practice was *Marananussati* 'Mindfulness of Death', one of the Forty Classical Meditations given by the Buddha Shakyamuni. We were instructed to organize our mundane affairs and establish a daily meditation schedule that would also include exercise, meals and his daily discourses and guidance.

At the end of the retreat, we expressed our deep gratitude and thanked Rinpoche for the profound teaching he had so generously given. He responded by saying we should thank ourselves for the good work we had done. Then turning to me he said, "It would be good to share this teaching with others."

A few years later, while at The Open Path in Boise Idaho, I finished transcribing and editing my notes of his discourses and published them.

During and since that time a growing interest in openly exploring the subject of death, as well as the process of dying, began to spread to the western world from the eastern schools of Buddhism where the classical meditation on Mindfulness of Death has been practiced for centuries. Many teachings and books on the subject emerged from both eastern and western worlds; all of immeasurable benefit in learning about death and dying both as inevitable event and as process in life.

Accepting the truth that we will die is not a morbid subject, as some may think, but actually the opposite. The real purpose of reflecting on death is to make an authentic, significant real-life change in our hearts and minds. Often this will require a period of retreat or contemplation, because only that can truly open our eyes to what we are doing with our lives, both inner and outer.

As our eyes open we are able to see and let go of unwholesome states that bind us to delusion and suffering and learn to foster wholesome states that open our hearts and minds. This is the way to transcend hope and fear, despair and distraction and allow loving kindness and compassionate wisdom to awaken and unfold so that we may experience the natural mind, our essential nature, peaceful, radiant, joyful, of benefit to oneself and others.

Although more than four decades have passed since Namgyal Rinpoche gave these discourses, they remain as timeless and as refreshing a guide to that transformation as they were then. In a pithy, clear and engaging manner, he illumines the themes of liberation through the practice of Mindfulness of Death as well as the quintessential practice of Mahamudra, the great sign that is no sign, inspiring us to practice them again and again to gain insight and deepen direct, unshakable realization of the truth of what is. This approach is particularly productive if done in retreat, especially when guided by a spiritual teacher (an invaluable resource for liberation), corresponding as it does to the light in which these discourses were originally given. Those not familiar with the formal practice of meditation but who pursue question relating to death, as well as to the infinite mysteries of life, will find his teaching provocative, relevant and helpful to their search, whatever form it takes.

Though he has passed on, it is with deep gratitude to the Venerable Namgyal Rinpoche and his compassionate, wise and skillful teaching of deliverance from suffering and the dispelling of delusion, that this second edition is respectfully offered for the welfare of all beings.

The Setting

In August 1976, Namgyal Rinpoche led a three-week meditation retreat at the request of eight students who, several weeks earlier, had travelled with him to the island of Crete. The meditation he chose for us to practice was *Marananussati* 'Mindfulness of Death'. During the retreat, we camped in a farmer's field that was separated from the sea and its long, narrow beach by small trees and shrubs. Nearby was a small river flowing gently to the sea, some bamboo thickets and a dry stubble field where grain had recently grown. Although we soon discovered that our chosen site was the local villagers' favourite beach, still, we were able to quietly and naturally continue meditating and simply integrated their sporadic comings and goings into the practice. Because of the heat, the discourses were held early in the morning under the shade of a tall thicket of bamboo.

Instructed by Rinpoche to prepare for the meditation period by relaxing and loosening the body, most of us began each day at dawn with a swim in the warm sea followed by a brisk, refreshing dip in the cold river to wash off sea salt. After breakfast we tidied up camp and returned to our tents to collect pens, notebooks and cushions.

The call went out as soon as Rinpoche's car was seen turning off the country road onto the dirt track leading to our campsite. By the time it travelled past the tethered nanny goats in the farmer's field and arrived, we had all gathered to greet him and pay our respects.

After emerging from the car, Rinpoche made his way to the shady spot where a mat and cushion had been placed on the ground for him and sat down. As the morning sun glistened through the leaves of the bamboo thicket behind him, he requested a rosary. All was silent except for our quiet murmuring as we joined him in reciting the mantra of Chenrezi, the great embodiment of compassion: OM MANI PADME HUM 'Hail to the Jewel in the Lotus'. Thus each day's discourse began.

1
Marananussati 'Mindfulness of Death'

The meditation on *Marana* 'death and compassion' or 'impermanence and compassion' is an ancient practice from the Mon tradition of Burma. In the Forty Classical Meditations given by the Buddha over 2,500 years ago, there are three groupings of ten, two groupings of four, and one grouping of two. *Marananussati* is listed in the third group of ten.

The first group of ten consists of meditation on the *Kasinas* in the following order: Earth, Water, Fire, Air, Blue, Yellow, Red, White, Space and Consciousness.

The second group of ten is on the *Asubha* 'that which is loathsome or not beautiful'. These are the meditations on the stages of decomposition of a corpse, sometimes called the Cemetery Meditations.

In the third group of ten there are meditations on

- *The Buddha* 'The Enlightened One'
- *The Dhamma* 'The Laws of Enlightenment'
- *The Sangha* 'The Community of Enlightened Beings'
- *Dana* 'Generosity'
- *Sila* 'Virtue'
- *Devas* 'Angels, Radiant Beings'

- *Marananussati* 'Mindfulness of Death'
- *Kayagata* 'Thirty-two Parts of the Body'
- *Anapanassati* 'Mindfulness of Breathing'
- *Upasama* 'Peace of Nibbana'

The fourth group consists of meditation on

- *The Brahma Vihara* 'Divine Abidings': Loving Kindness, Compassion, Transcendent Joy and Equanimity
- *Arupa-Bhava* 'Formless Spheres of Existence': Infinite Space, Infinite Consciousness, Infinite Nothingness, Neither Perception nor Non-Perception'

The last group consists of meditation on

- *Ahara* 'Nutriment, food': Material, (Sensorial and Mental) Impression, Mental Volition, Consciousness
- *Catu-Dhatu-Vavatthana* 'Analysis of the Four Elements': Earth, Water, Fire, Air

The first six meditations of the third group are not given to beginners because path experience must come first. One needs to be grounded in this experience, then one can practise them. This third group is called the *Anussati* meditations. *Sati* means 'mindfulness' and *anu*—like the English words 'anew' and 'renew'—means 'to remember, to recollect or to review' something again and again until you have further and deeper insights into the subject. It is not a visual experience but a use of the intellect to get past intellectual concepts.

Marananussati 'Mindfulness of Death' is the practice of bringing the mind back to reflect again and again on the theme of death. Normally, the word *mara* 'death' does not appear alone in Buddhist texts; it usually appears as *jati-mara* 'birth-death' and is seen as a temporary ending to a temporary phenomenon. It's not considered permanent. So *Marananussati* is really a meditation that preserves and increases energy and, ultimately, compassion.

The question you must ask is: *Why is this bubble of energy going to dissolve?* It is also a question of karma, to find out the life span of a being. So *Marananussati* is a specific question not only of why, but also of when.

The Abhidhamma states that there are two types of death:

1. Timely death, where a person has 'x' amount of energy to maintain the life and that is used up.
2. Untimely death, where there is enough life energy but it is cut off by a catastrophe, as in war or an accident.

There are many energy bases in a life and one uses them up rather like different flavours of soup: first you use up the asparagus soup, then the tomato soup and so on. Once the karmic foundation of life is formed it is operative; when it is exhausted there is then the opportunity to form another energy base. This is what occurs at conception.

Because your energy affects what you study, you must be unafraid when you begin this meditation so that you can study death dispassionately. Many questions will arise; for example, in untimely death where the energy is not exhausted: *How then will this energy be used up?* Depth consideration of this may provide explanations for many infant deaths, for example, that occur, seemingly, for no reason. Perhaps what appears to be an untimely death is, in fact, a timely one. So this meditation is concerned with the study of karma and not with despair. In fact, you might say the enemy of this meditation is the weeping, wailing and gnashing of teeth. It is better to use your energy to gain insight into death and to further your progress on the path.

The following *Anussati* meditations balance each other. Meditation on:

The Triple Gem—*the Buddha, Dharma and Sangha*—develops faith.
The Thirty-two Parts of the Body develops non-clinging, objectivity.
Death develops energy and effort and eliminates despair.
Peace develops loving-kindness.

Faith
is balanced by
Effort. Non-clinging
is balanced by Loving-kindness.
If there's too much faith, you are not
getting on with the work. If there's too much
love, there's too much sensuality or exclusiveness.
If there's too much aversion or despair, take
Refuge in The Triple Gem or the
GURU

No matter how glorious your life is, death is a fact.

Beings who are ego-oriented never get over their aversions; they are anti-people, anti-life, and they never get down to the bedrock of compassion.

Ask the questions: *Why be compassionate?*

How can one be compassionate?

This meditation on death can cultivate a spontaneous automatic involvement with living compassion; but, to make the Teaching living, *you* must die.

In the practice of *Marananussati* you simply raise the question of death. Bring the mind back to this theme again and again to increase the bundle of doubt. All these manifestations are going to die. See this clearly with detachment. Be ye not moved. From that come the questions: *Why? What is dying? Is it an ego formation that dies? Is it the cells that die? Or do they go on?* Then, maybe, from this question making you can have a dialogue with death.

> Walk, stand, sit and lie with death.
> Look around you . . .
> The bamboo thicket that you see
> represents the tangle of the mind.
> The only way to transcend death
> is to look at the tangle dispassionately.
> If you understand death,
> you will understand energy
> and you will see how to use it
> more effectively on the path.

You can make anxiety a deliberate tool: meditate in a precarious position, in a tree or at the edge of a cliff. In this posture keep sounding: *What is death?*

Only in death is there no posture.

2
Concentration Is Present

Your eyes are always moving. Every moment is composed of thousands of pinpoints of light. When all is swallowed to one point—which occurs frequently in insight practice—you are at the threshold of the mystical experience: *God has left a little point betwixt He and Thee.*

In *Vajrayana* practice there is an experience—symbolized by *Vajradhara* 'the holder of the diamond state of consciousness'—of a diamond-blue point of light. You can judge the depth of this state by its brilliance.

Whatever practice it occurs in, *Samatha* or *Vipassana*, this swallowing of the consciousness to one point is followed by the experience of a hundred thousand eyes, the cells of the body directly knowing. It is thrilling and blissful and is the actual nature of mind speaking.

The *Abhidhamma* states that in every moment of consciousness *samadhi* 'concentration' is present. Your work is not so much to establish concentration but to experience the concentration that is already there. Although the mind may become distracted, if you are calm the concentration will be fairly easy to find and gradually you will be able to sustain and increase its span. Concentration does not take effort, the development of calm absorption, however, does. If you can deepen the diamond-blue point of light you will make rapid progress. This point is not necessarily visual; you can experience it physically as well. You may even hear it.

There are many stages of bliss enumerated in the classical texts. They differ basically in the degree of intensity of experience. However, all bliss has many points undulating, vibrating. This is law. It is in the range of human consciousness. At the beginning of the spiritual life you want to experience everything, but then you will want to choose what will unfold you most rapidly and skillfully. This is the most compassionate, the most wholesome thing to do.

3
Siddhartha, A Symbol of Every Man

The Prince Siddhartha is a symbol of everyman in that every being is like a prince. In Christianity there is a tendency to view human life as impoverished, whereas in Buddhism this lifetime is considered precious and rare. All human beings are surrounded by riches and living in a palace, as did Siddhartha for the first part of his life. But one day he saw someone who was very ill, and then he saw old age, decay and death. These are called the first three messengers or signs. He realized that nothing he could give his wife and child would prevent them from meeting this same fate. Then he saw the fourth sign, a holy man. From his love for his family came the desire to find the gift that is beyond death.

As soon as you are born you start to decay. You cannot give anything to anyone unless you transcend illness, old age, decay and death. As long as you have a house you have death; as long as you have a body you have death; as long as you have senses you have death. *What is the gift that can be given?* Maybe it's a transmission that is no transmission.

Reflect on Siddhartha and his life and you might see that this rich life is not enough. The renunciation that comes from this teaching is not negative. We are in a palace, the body, where we can experience exciting things, but that is not enough for the development of compassion. Like Siddhartha, you must find that which is beyond death, to transmute or resolve it, to find that which builds the palace. There is a Koan: *How do you get the goose out of the bottle without breaking the bottle or killing the goose?* The goose is a symbol of Buddha-nature. The foundation for the holy life is to reflect: *Not enough! Lacking!* You must ask, *What is lacking?* Work with these koans to establish the foundation for the holy life.

Shakyamuni is sometimes experienced as a field of gold or radiating golden light, symbolizing wholesome karma. *Muni* means 'sage, profound being of merit'. It's wise to be wise. It's healing to be wise.

Death is that to which all things are hurtling. You have no time to waste. If there is intellectualization or verbalization, use it on one theme and then gradually the need for verbalization will die away. Repeatedly focusing your intellect on a subject is bound to bring insight. Gradually you will become quieter and will drop verbalization, but not intelligence.

Use the mantra MARANA or OM MANI PADME HUM to develop compassion and a truly beautiful life. If you meditate on the beautiful you cannot help but be beautiful. *A rose is a rose is a rose* ... as Gertrude Stein said. And a stein, after all, is something to drink out of.

4
Three Characteristics of Existence

There is a point where the ego experiences death. Once there is the transcendence of the ego, then cellular death can be experienced objectively because the dying process is carried in every cell of the organism. The cells of the body die and transmute, so it is possible to die and to live.

You would know it as soon as the ego died . . . that's what you're worried about . . . *you* dying. But we are not studying the death of you. The transcendence of your image is necessary to really study death.

> You must transcend the being that is studying—the questioner—and become the question. Then the real meditation can begin. See what is dying around you. All things are arising and ceasing, undulating and interpenetrating. Make a note as to how you are seeing, how you are perceiving.

Death can be seen as *Anicca, Dukkha* and *Anatta,* the three characteristics of being or existence.

> *Anicca* is 'impermanence' everything is in constant flux.

Dukkha is 'suffering' the unsatisfactoriness or the continuous struggle of life, the gaining and losing.

Anatta is 'not-self' the impersonality of all existence.

Look at the stalk of bamboo, at the branch, at the leaf. How do you perceive them? Do you see changing, or do you see losing and augmenting? Or is it *anatta*, 'gone-ness' or 'God-ness' that you see?

[To illustrate this Rinpoche picked up three objects and lightly tossed them into the air in front of us, one at a time. The first, a small splinter of wood, flickered rapidly as it fell to the ground.]

Anicca 'Fast changes'.

[The second object—a stone—landed on the ground with a thud.]

Dukkha 'Heaviness'.

[The third object—a small, dry piece of straw—wafted weightlessly to the ground like golden sunlight.]

Anatta 'Gone-ness'.

Notice these three characteristics until they become feeling states. Don't try to work it out with the intellect because by the time the experience gets to the intellect it is too late. Let the experience sort itself out. Ask yourself: *How do you experience?*

With the direct realization of each of these three characteristics, there is joy. That's when you become the stalk of bamboo you are meditating on. And even when the joy arises, it's business as usual; continue to practice detachment and simply observe.

5
Wisdom and Compassion

Question: How do I deal with frustration when I am disturbed or distracted in the meditation?

There is frustration because of the fact that most beings, including you, are not operating at a full mandala capacity. Suffering is a fact. Observe it coolly. Do not become emotionally involved. The only compassionate thing to do is to awaken. You can't do anything in an unenlightened state except raise the question: *Is there something beyond disease, old age and death?*

You are not required to believe in a saviour. All you are required to believe is there is Guru, an 'x' factor, God, that which is beyond death, beyond the intellect, beyond words. This is the only point of faith. The rest is the development of wisdom and compassion. Wisdom is clear seeing, knowing there is disease, old age, decay and death and the acceptance of that as a fact. Despair and emotionalism are the enemies of meditation. Although it is good to reflect on suffering, you must avoid projecting your own frustrations of not getting this or that on to it. It is not good to brood over and over again. Morbidity is caused by the repetition of blind, habitual patterns. You must make the effort to break out of these patterns, like continually complaining about an unhappy childhood. Okay, if that was the case, once you've got that message move on; because you know, when you throw manure against the wind you only get it right back in the face.

At the *Samana* stage of development there is the experience of serenity and compassion. In the realm of impermanence, you are decaying; have a calm acceptance of that fact, not resignation. Wisdom and compassion are your greatest tools. Then there is a way allied with these. It is the way of simplicity and is found in the clarity of the senses: sitting simply on the earth, touching, hearing, seeing, smelling, tasting. Fear of death is based on a mind product of beings that are divorced from nature. Immerse yourself in the simplicity of nature and it will bring you to accept death calmly, as a fact. This is the way to pass beyond. This calm acceptance is not an emotional plop, but accepting the thoughts, accepting the lost-ness. Whoever experienced found-ness? When beings are calm they experience the beautiful, which is beyond death. It is the reflection of a wholesome state.

> Just listen to the story.
> Listen to the process going on.
> Say neither *Yea* nor *Nay*.
> Every moment is provocation . . .
> To be . . . or not to be?
> To be is to hover, like a butterfly.
> There is the transcendence . . .

When everything is disturbing you, perhaps you are disturbance. The ego is the pattern of decisions you have made about the disturbance, about duality. The ego-view is built of yes's and no's. You are a product of impermanence so long as you say, *This, is disturbing*.

> Duality is disturbing.
> You are disturbing.
> All is disturbing!

But there are the two breasts of *Tara* which hang down to be nearer to the earth so that beings can suckle.

You are breathed . . . sounded . . . smelled . . . tasted . . . touched . . . The karmic energy causes breath, *prana*, the movement of the sea.

> The resistance is not your resistance.
> You can't breathe without resistance.
> Does the tree decide to uproot itself?

The tree uproots and blows across the desert. The tumbleweed is the juggler, the fool. This is the stage in the awakening when Shakyamuni said, *I have found you, Oh Builder, you will build no more*. This is a very personal statement.

Cast down is the ridge pole! . . . the spine in your house, the body, the place of refuge that you try and try to erect. But when the vertical becomes horizontal you become one with the ground of being. *Done is that which had to be done. For this there is no more subject to becoming.* This is the point where you no longer resist the resistance.

To call these statements of Shakyamuni's a symbol is too deadening a word. It's not just seeing a pretty picture of the spiritual life. They are actually a mind experience that has texture and quality. There is the sense that a human task has been fulfilled.

In one of Kazantzakis's novels, the central character says to God, *Use me . . . but not too much*. Later he says, *Use me . . . but don't break me*. Finally, he says, *Use me . . . who cares!*

**Keep your eyes on God, on Awakening,
for there is death in all things,
even in Tantra.**

6
Symbols at Death

Q: There was a vision in the meditation of a square sheet of cloth with ragged edges. It had a circular opening in the centre, and air, like snowflakes, passed through. What meaning does this have?

Two things occur at death: the summation symbol—the sign of karmic rebirth—and the veil. Usually the symbol appears on the veil.

The *Tara* initiation is always accompanied by a veil and is a sign of protection. The snowflakes are the *Vajrasattva* experience of purification. Meditate on *Vajrasattva* 'the Great Cleanser': OM VAJRASATTVA AH, the first mantra given out by Guru Rinpoche. The colours of the cloth or veil are also significant: white edges indicate purity; rainbow threads are the grace waves of Lama-mind. The veil is the tapestry of life, which is very much an actuality. In this case it is not yet complete.

7
The Only Refuge Is Freedom

When you are taking refuge, perhaps your motivation is hope that is driven by fear, so really that is no refuge. The only refuge is freedom, abiding where there is no abiding. Then you can speak of real refuge.

The essence of the teaching is peace, *nirvana, anatta*; and this can only be attained by the experience of that which is beyond death. *Samsara* is wandering, now here, now there, driven willy-nilly, wanting this, rejecting that. It is driven by fear and all fear is fear of losing the ego.

Aspire to abide where there is no abiding. Once the experience beyond death manifests, then we can talk of compassion; otherwise we bandy about neuroses.

In the meditation today work on the theme of non-refuge and non-clinging and see their relationship. The greatest sin in the teaching is *avijja* 'non-seeing'. Know that refuge is not here, not there, not in the illusory refuges of fame, power, wealth, not even in spiritual materialism. To speak of Lama Refuge is something else; it is beyond the ordinary refuge and cannot be found in a particularized place or thing. This Lama Refuge is *Samma-Ditthi* 'Complete View, Complete Seeing'.

Short of path experience everything is non-seeing. Even hankering after enlightenment is still non-seeing. Replace the desire for refuge with the realization of refuge. Meditate on:

Those who save themselves will lose themselves, and those who lose themselves will save themselves.

This is the realization of true refuge and purification, of non-clinging awareness. This is well expressed by the epitaph on Kazantzakis' tombstone: *No hope. No fear. Free!* To prefer is to be driven by hope and fear. Non-discrimination or choiceless awareness is the essence of dharma, which is not afraid to make a choice—unlike some beings who are too security oriented to select. Listen to the story being received by the five *skandhas*; be aware of the dharma you are!

Done is that which had to be done. In this statement by Gautama Buddha, there is the sense of a great task that has been completed. There is the same feeling in Christ's statement while on the Cross: *It is finished.*

If you don't have an impossible task you are an impossible human being. Every being should attempt what is impossible, what is beyond them. Supreme Awakening? . . . as far as the ego is concerned? . . . Impossible!

8
Choiceful Awareness

As nature ascends on the evolutionary scale, there begins to develop a concept of death. The ape draws back from the exposed skull of a dead ape because it sees impermanence. You have concern about the ego and so you have concern about death. Why not meet the concept of your own death? Nature is aware of its going. You cannot maintain the previous *you*.

Angst is a systematic alertness, the ego in a pure state, which screens all things. It is simply the watcher, the Janus principle, the screener, filer and evaluator. The ego arises in any form of life wherever there is *nama-rupa* 'mind and form'. Sheep have screeners too, so don't bother transcending the ego, make it viable. Develop Aryan pride; strengthen it as a useful tool for seeing the ongoing choosing.

But there is also a going beyond, not listening for or against, but listening. Even after the experience of path there is ego. Choiceless awareness brings the experience of *choiceful* awareness. Peripheral vision, in a sense, is non-ego, and the ego is that which selects or brings into focus. You can't avoid it, you are selectivity, but you can select peripheral consciousness. That's why you can say *choiceful* awareness.

**Awareness involves choices.
It's the first and last freedom.**

Awareness is seeing the ongoing choice making. Instead of saying: *I cannot meditate,* say *Meditation must occur.* Use the theme of the meditation as a question maker. Listen to the whole story—the weavings—and the reality of meditation will become effortless, like listening to the birds. Listen to all the efforts and the effort making will be gone.

9
Awakening Consciousness Is Present

Q: When I am involved in wholesome activity the ego seems to disappear, joy and serenity are present. But when there is just observing, there arises nothing but I . . . I . . . I . . . Wouldn't it be better to be hammered into gold rather than try to hammer the gold? There is difficulty in both situations but, for me, the activity is easier to live with. In action there is both knowing and unknowing, but in this 'sitting and watching' there is only unknowing.

Freud referred to the process of Buddhist meditation as planned schizophrenia because there is a deliberate removal of sensory contact and the ego-identification gradually becomes nonfunctional. The nature of consciousness requires an object.

Introverts are egocentric and are only concerned with *How do things affect me?* and *How do I affect them?* As they try harder and harder to save themselves they gradually become nonfunctional because they lack sensory contact.

Their opposite, the extroverts, become lost in the duties of daily life, in sense fulfillment and mechanical routines. Generally, they don't like to ask questions about themselves.

The only way to find liberation is through both *pancadvara* 'the sense-door' and *manodvara* 'the mind-door'. Then consciousness becomes the supreme object, the watcher. Before there is observation, consciousness arises and passes through a subject-object relationship of the ego without awareness. When awareness is established then consciousness watches what is taken by mind for the object, the story-making, the verbalization, the concept-making. Consciousness, with infinite patience watches what arises. Be aware of this process going on. Awakening consciousness is present. Change your observation from *I am doing this*, to *This is happening*. Who are you anyway? There is no *you*. The life story, which is concerned with consciousness, has nothing to do with *you*.

> Watch whatever arises, as you would watch
> strangers across the street.

You can use mantra as an aid. There are three types of mantra. One type is all seed syllables:

> The emphasis is on sound not form.
> The electric hum . . . OM AH HUM . . .
> like the sound of seashells.
> Wherever there is forming
> there is sounding . . . communication.

The second type of mantra is a mixture of seed syllables and words:

> OM MANI PADME HUM.
> All soundings of the universe
> are the divine formings.
> All matter is a flowering jewel.
> All nature is an act of compassion.
> Think of the compassion of the grass.
> Think of the compassion of the cow.
> Transcend *your* practice of compassion
> and become an embodiment of compassion.
> Wherever there is form, there is solace.

This brings us to the third type of mantra, which evokes the intellect:

> OM GATE GATE PARAGATE PARASAMGATE BODHI SVAHA!
> You are the crown of existence that is
> unfolding into pure diamond-mind intelligence.
> Basically, all is going!
>
> Everyone's life is a collecting of sticks, stones and straw.
>
> Everything is chaff before the Awakening.
>
> But the experience of Buddhahood is the wheat.

This process of planned schizophrenia is a technique to produce the golden wheat of Buddhahood. What you have to work with is the hollow stalk, the central channel. But the stalk is not the wheat. Do you want to know how to grow a mushroom? You take the stalk and place it in the manure; the spores travel up the stalk and . . .

Your work is never to give up the question. So keep on gathering the manure. The good farmer wants to know how much shit she or he has. Recollect, keep on collecting the shit. Let it pile up. Eventually it will make a fire, burn the dross, and transmute into gold. The spores are everywhere. You will experience the fire. Don't worry, I am here.

10
Awaken the Clarity

Q: What do you do when you experience calm but there isn't any energy?

Too many beings have the sin of quietism. Do the meditation on *Milarepa*; it will produce joy and bring energy.

One of the Sixteen Stages of Insight is 'Calm Clarity with Energy'. Make the effort to gradually introduce energy into the meditation by the practice of awareness. You will experience emptiness and hollowness, light will fill the body and a great joy will pervade your being. Awaken the clarity. The two-in-one truth is to use the energy to awaken the awakening.

You cannot transcend duality until you have reduced everything to Death.

11
Dreams and Visions

Q: How does one work with symbols and dreams or visions that arise during meditation?

There is an orderly progression of awareness in working with dreams and visions. Recall as much as you possibly can while it is still fresh. Don't try to beat it into consciousness if it doesn't arise spontaneously. Instead, listen to it, hear it in depth; feel it more and you will be able to bring what is unconscious to a conscious level. Recall will bring you to feelings, then to associations, and then to insights. Avoid interpreting these verbally because the insights can even transcend words. Then, after the experience, if necessary, you can verbalize.

A symbol is highly impacted with teachability. For instance, if you were to meditate on a corpse—which is one of the Forty Classical Meditations—you would attain only the first level of *Jhana* 'blissful absorption', whereas meditation on a cluster of eggs or crystals is capable of unfolding you to the fourth stage of *Jhana* 'serene at-one-ment'. If you wished to go further you would do the meditation on formlessness.

Which vision or dream will be most beneficial for you to work on? You will know when you have it. Its importance will be self-evident. Re-examine the vision/dream, usually from the end to its beginning. Seal it by review, then let it go. You can take a definitive vision and give it a meditative session. Ask depth questions about its nature.

The greater the vision or dream is, the more you must work it; use it as a meditation until it is smooth, until it is incorporated into your being.

12
Technique

Q: Is technique important for successful practice?

Technique has its place but it's more important to have confidence at first. In Dream Yoga, for example, it's important to be comfortable and have a straight spine. If you're new to this type of yoga, then relaxation, especially, is the priority. Later you may pick up better ways of doing it. It's much like a progression at school: for example, in first year science you study slides of someone else's work, the next year you make your own slides. When you want to explore more deeply, then technique will be important. Once you've got the interest you will be willing to struggle with the focus.

You are a genius, but what does the genius love? Notice the connection between genius and genesis. Are you interested in your origins? If you are, the discipline should be an effortless joy.

13
The Practice of Mahamudra

In beginning the practice of Mahamudra you first put the emphasis on developing calm. Then awaken the calm; this is called Bright Awareness. Second, practise awareness in daily life. Practise joy, it will produce interest and interest always increases joy. Practise awareness today by following the movements of body, speech and mind. Develop equilibrium by balancing the body, by loosening it, and slow the breathing down. Breath is speech; it's the primary communication. Then relax and loosen the mind. Don't cling to or rely on any thought or idea. Let everything go—even the thought of salvation.

> Remain in a natural state
> not taking or leaving anything.
> Let the senses and thoughts flow by themselves
> without hindering them.
> To reject, to discriminate,
> is to be for or against.
> This is all *tanha* 'clinging'.
> Drop the concept of enlightenment.
> Practise Mahamudra and give up concepts
> and clinging for seven days.

Follow the practice in an orderly way by relaxing the body, slowing down the breath, and then very easefully stripping the mind of all concepts. Watch them go—the ideas of you, God, enlightenment—then enter the illumined state of mind. Allow the risings and fallings of dharma to flow and purify of their own accord as in a bubbling, narrowing or widening stream. Just say, *Yet another illusion* . . . but don't get nasty with it, it's important not to make a judgment about the illusion. In this state *samadhi* 'concentration' and activity are one.

Samma-Samadhi 'Complete-Concentration' or *Jhana* 'Absorption' has five factors. First there is *vitakka* 'initial application or focus'. For this you may use an object or a mandala. Second, there is *vicara* 'sustained application or scanning', the investigation of the object. This produces the third factor, *piti* 'physical bliss, joy, interest, discovery'. The fourth is *sukha* 'happiness', the consummation of the object, the transformation. The word *sukha* comes from *su*, meaning 'going to good'; *kha* means 'space' and refers also to the primordial sound of the crow flying into boundless space; and *ha* is 'laughter, letting go'. *Sukha* is 'all-rounded easefulness', the blackness flying away.

The fifth factor is *upekkha* 'detachment, equanimity, or higher standing, dwelling in oneness': complete incorporated continuity, nonattached awareness. In this stage there is no emotional experience. It is complete ease, like wearing comfortable clothing. It is sometimes referred to as *ekaggata* 'one-going, boundlessness, serenity'. This is not the spaced-out feeling that drug users refer to. This boundlessness is bright awareness. That is why drugs are rejected in the teaching; they do not produce a natural, clear and total experience.

Allow the contraction and expansion of the mantra OM AH HUM to balance body, speech and mind. Allow the slow and fast cycles of mental states and karmic patterns to occur and observe them with effortless effort.

14
Working with Question

Before you go into meditation, it is quite legitimate to have a question, no matter what the meditation. But it must be a question that you feel your consciousness could be meaningfully involved in. There's a vast range of questions that could invite investigation.

When a breakthrough comes there is a calm absorption accompanied by the awareness of the question. This may bring a quick succession of insights. During the meditation you may not be aware of the connections so it's important to take five to ten minutes at the end of each session to review the main stream as well as specific symbols that arose. If something happened or a symbol appeared, you may want to question it further during the review. It's also very good to see the relative successes or errors of each meditation session in a dispassionate way . . . *This arose and fell*. Be economical and brief.

Keep the main theme to sharpen the mind. The main body of the meditation is the question set by the teacher. Like a koan, it is the hook or peg on which you can hang a few garments. Whenever you don't know what to do in the meditation, go back to the koan or theme.

> *Except a man be born again,*
> *he shall not see the Kingdom of Heaven.*

> *You must at some time grapple with the Angel of Death*

> *Return your bones to your Father and your flesh to your Mother.*

Unless you realize that life is a repetition of arising and passing away, you will never reach maturity.

> Do your scales: Doh Re Mi . . .
> Unless you pursue the theme,
> unless you do the scales,
> you won't have the dough,
> you won't have the ray,
> and you won't see me!
> Do your scales
> and you will have music!

15
Four Levels of Understanding Dharma

[Hunting season arrived on Crete bringing amateur sportsmen to our campsite area. Lacking real game, they sometimes satisfied themselves with taking potshots at the small birds in the trees . . . under which one of us would happen to be meditating. Their lack of safety precautions and inaccurate aim added a note of realism to the meditation on death and prompted the following question:]

Q: What is the dharma of guns?

You have an ego concept of guns. There are four levels of understanding dharma. First there is good and evil on opposite sides. Second, they become allies. Third, they then become one. And fourth, even that one does not exist.

> All beings are hunting and being hunted . . .
> But the hunter doesn't necessarily partake of the hunted.

16
Putting Down Verbalization

Westerners have difficulty putting down verbalization, whether it is chitter-chatter, intellectualization, or evaluation of their thoughts. Nevertheless, the meditation on death will reduce you to true humility—humus, earth.

The Teaching is *Samma-Sambuddha* 'Complete Awakening, Complete Knowing'. How long do you think it would take you to know everything there is to know about bamboo? It would take a lifetime by any of the normal processes of education, the study of biology, laboratory analysis, verbalization and so on, a lifetime to know the complete story. I am reminded of a brilliant scientist and scholar who at the age of eighty, knowing death was imminent, felt bitter and frustrated. He realized that in the vast range of all there is to know and discover in his field of study he had barely begun, in spite of his dedicated effort.

Meditation shows you how profitless it is to debate the mysteries of life with the intellect. This method is fruitless as well as erroneous.

Even if you have good views, because they are conditional, you must distrust them. Notice I didn't say 'dishonour'; but you must realize that your view is relative and therefore subject to error. So logically you must go from the intellect to something more fundamental. You must go to the depth, down below thought, into the humus of your being.

> Consciousness dwells in non-distinction.
> Words are only the flowers of the tree.
> And the Tree of Life is best studied in the autumn
> when all the flowers and leaves have fallen.
> You must find the source of the words.
>
> You are a walking plant, a walking tree.
> So go down to the messages of the cells,
> the messages of the nervous system.
> These are the roots of the flower of the intellect.
>
> Putting down the intellect is not negative . . .
> this tree has many flowers . . .
> But it has to be transmuted into pure hearing,
> pure seeing, smelling, tasting, touching . . .
> Unless you find the source
> it will not tell you the whole story.

Don't cling to views. *Miccha-Ditthi* is 'erroneous view' and therefore in error; but even *ditthi* 'view', because it is partial, is also subject to error. This meditation on death shows that the intellect, as you know it, is partial and conditional. You cannot build *Samma-Ditthi* 'Total View' with it even though you may get connections.

**You have to seek the pure raw source
of intelligence making.**

Death, like a sword, will cut off the partial view of the intellect. The Buddha speaks of cutting through the undergrowth, the words and thoughts, like cutting off the hairs on the head. Listen past the intellect and the senses; get down to the skull.

> Don't be trapped in the produce of the mind.
> In the beginning you do have to see
> the produce, the cabbages.
> Then you have to see the garden.
> And then you have to see the gardener.

There is the Teaching *That Though Art*. But this is also beyond conceptualization yet does not reject conceptualization. A hair's breadth sets heaven and earth apart. Do not weigh up the fruits of verbalization but go down deeper, see the whole tree. You cannot see it if you are an ant on one of the leaves.

See every being as your mother. See every event as your father. See how your relative mind is formed. See there is nothing there that is *you* exclusively. You are more the child watching it all, impressed by it all. If you didn't let the impressions carry you away, you would grow up.

You could say there are five stages in growing up. The first is the child with mouth open, the mud pie stage in which no apparent change is perceived. This is okay in the realm of tranquillity meditation.

In the second stage there is the perception of changing and being changed. This could be described as the older child wielding a wooden stick beginning to affect at least gross changes.

The third stage sees only changes. There is a refinement of tools, a finer discrimination and the awareness of being 'worked'. This insight will eventually lead to the fourth stage, the experience of changelessness. This is the day of graduation to responsible adulthood.

If you don't cling you will go beyond these four to the fifth stage, the abiding in the non-abiding. This is the full citizenship into the awakened community, which includes the realization of the validity of the previous four stages but neither accepts nor rejects them.

**Keep your eyes on the fifth stage.
Duality is as illusive a dharma as any other.**

Q: In meditation there was the seeing of hands and feet of a skeleton in a mirror, also one skull vanishing to reveal another. What does this mean?

Continue to ask about these principles of hands and feet. The mirror is crystal consciousness and there is its opposite, black velvet, on the other side. Note the alternation of consciousness between these two. Try to ask nonverbal questions as these experiences arise. The mirror practice is one of *Maya-Yoga* where crystal consciousness is the focus. Forms may appear without a form. Do not now, however, concentrate on mirrors for insight.

In the Sixteen Buddha-body practice, the *Dukkha-Cariya*, skeleton level, is the teacher of suffering and dispassion. This is sometimes portrayed in Buddhist paintings of Shakyamuni in a cave, near starvation with his skeleton visible through his skin. There are seven layers of experiencing the skulls and you must pass through all of them. When you transcend the intellect the insights come faster. You cannot afford the non-luxury of verbalization . . . *Can it be this? Could it be that?* This process is stagnant and must be dropped.

The lesson of Virgo is the dying of over-elaboration in order to realize simple light, the ground of being. Train yourself to ask nonverbal questions and eventually you will get through to simplicity. Then, from the ground of being, you can elaborate.

There will always be in the consciousness the *Yes, No,* the wanting to jump into the abyss of the unknown and the holding back from the light. It is blinding. You cannot look face to face with God and live. In fact, you cannot look face to face with a blade of grass and live!

> Somewhere in the breath *you* are not breathing.
> Find it.
> That's death.

> Do *Pranayama*.
> The radiant orb burns up the netted undergrowth,
> the cross-relationships.
> They're hindrances.
> What hindrances?

17
Meditation Posture

Q: In sitting in the lotus posture there is a buildup of energy to establish calm concentration. Is there some way to do this in a prone position or are there other positions that may be used?

Yes, there is the Lion posture. Lie on your right side, left leg on top of the right leg, left arm resting on the left side of the body and the right hand cupped under the right ear. A pillow can be used to raise the head and shoulder, the spine and head are aligned and straight and the knees slightly bent. But this may be uncomfortable for a Westerner so you can do the Corpse posture. Lie on your back with your arms and legs slightly extended so that you form a five-pointed star. This is very good for the Tara meditation. The eyes in the hands and the third eye form a triangle.

I don't think it's good for Westerners to sit in the lotus posture too much. It's like aping their betters or what they think are their betters. There are many postures that can be used for meditation. In fact, the Buddha gave instructions to divide the day equally between the four major postures: walking, standing, sitting and lying down. In some meditations it's one hour of walking to one hour of sitting. Sometimes a quick run around the Temple is done between the changes of the two postures. There are different forms for different reasons.

You can stand. You can lie in the sun; but know what you are doing. Normally I don't recommend a prone meditation posture to Western students as they tend to fall asleep in this position because of their conditioning. I would say that you should explore lying down in the star position in the sunlight, and the standing position, for half an hour at a time. In standing, you can lean against a wall, for example. But you must be careful; don't just do it for some result. Be aware of the whole process. You must know what you are doing!

If I took this stone *[Rinpoche picked up a stone]* and were to throw it at you *[he suddenly threw it at the student]* . . . What caught the stone?

Student: *[catching the stone at heart level]* My heart!

Did not your hands catch it too? Didn't your whole being catch the stone?

18
Discipline—A Path to Union

The word discipline comes from disciple, a follower of truth. People too often view discipline as a set of rules that must be followed rigidly. This is too harsh an interpretation. Discipline is not a set of rules or a technique. It is a yoga, a yoke, a binding. The deep meaning of discipline is union. It is a path to union, to making oneself over into union. Discipline is harmonizing, following the truth, not a concept or an order from someone but a training of oneself into harmony. It's making an effort but it's not *You must do this*, but rather, *This must be done*. The precepts taken by Buddhists are used as a mental training in compassion.

The yoke is also loosening the flow of God, for if one is bound to God one is free. Christ said to Peter: *Thou art Petros, upon this rock I will build my church*. *Petros*, the Greek word for a 'small pebble' and the word *petra* 'rock or foundation' are similar in symbolic meaning to the Sanskrit word *padma* 'lotus, primordial purity' foundation of enlightenment. Change the pebble into the rock of stability upon which the church, the experiencing of the universe, can be built. The dialogue is between the pebble and the rock, the microcosm and macrocosm, freedom and union. The pebble, like the mustard seed, refers to kundalini at the base of the spine; the rock is the divine eye; birds singing along the spine are the harmony of the two.

Christ said to Peter: *I will give you the keys to the kingdom of heaven; whatever you bind on earth will be bound in heaven, and whatever you loose on earth will be loosed in heaven.* Note that 'keys' is plural. At the time of the Greek mysteries and the Qabbalah—the ancient Hebrew teaching—keys were shaped, not as they are now, but as bars or T's. In the Tarot the keys refer to the Hierophant, which represents loosening and binding. Realizations of what is building are the keys to the kingdom of heaven, divine union.

Symbols and parables are an economy of speech highly impacted with realization. When Jesus and the Buddha spoke in parables or symbolic language, many realizations were able to flow. So discipline yourself to follow a theme or koan; this is what will lead you from a binding to a loosening.

You must remember that the early Christians were in touch with the Greeks and had references to the Pythagorean mysteries. 'Kingdom' refers to that which is orderly and harmonious; . . . *and the gates of hell shall not prevail against it.* The 'gates of hell' refer to disharmony.

The ancient Kings of Israel look back to ancient times . . . They look back because the majesty that was once there is now lost or veiled, which Salome's dance of the seven veils hints at. Harmony is there but it is not perceived. There are shadows of glory but not the full kingdom.

You can only fulfill discipline in as much as you are in harmony. It is the path leading to the Path. The duty of the teacher, who is also a friend and a guide, is to set themes of reflection to lead a disciple to full realization.

In the Mysteries, the Master casts down the staff—the symbol of Will—and the disciple is ordered to pick it up. At first, no matter how the disciple does it, it is incorrect. Notice that the staff, as in the Hermit card of the Tarot, is a limb from a living tree. This represents the flowering will, the serpent, which may round on you, and if you are out of harmony, you are out. The idea is to bring the Will back to the kingdom, which is rich, majestic and orderly. Christ said, *I come not to break the law but to fulfill the law.* So when you pick up the staff, if you are in harmony you will fulfill the law.

How does your meditation reflect the universe? Is it a chip off the old block—*petra* 'a pebble' from the rock? In discipline it's the attitude that's important. Whoever can read their own being as a pebble, humble, will experience their foundation of harmony.

In the Tarot, the cards of the Emperor and the Empress, the Magician and the High Priestess also represent the dialogue of loosening and binding. There must be a dialogue between these two functions because if you are too bound you are rigid, and if you are too loose, you are scattered all over the place. Beings who resent discipline are in a state of disharmony; but in their depths they really want freedom *and* stability. You can only realize this state by following truth or letting it catch you.

The universe is bound, but it is also loose. The *Sambhogakaya* is the aspect of 'divine play'; the *Nirmanakaya* is the stability of the 'root-guru', the pebble, the flowing water in the centre of the rock. *Moses struck the rock with his staff and the waters poured forth.* Only when the rock is struck with Will can the waters flow forth and wash you white as snow. This is the dialogue of the red and white channels up the spine. The staff, or the central channel, represents stability, which comes from discipline; baptism is the flowering of freedom.

Christ said, *As Moses lifted up the serpent in the wilderness, even so must man be lifted up by love.* The desert is the wilderness of your mind. Paul said, *Though I speak with the tongues of men and of angels, but have not love, I have become as sounding brass* . . . Brass is imitative gold and copper is love. Your ego is as brass, only a reflection of the real glory. When the kingdom is realized the ego is transmuted into pure gold.

> You are surrounded by Will seeking to attain.
> The whole surface of the earth is sent forth
> from God unto God doing the impossible.
> It's only in the attempt to do the impossible
> that you experience God.
> In that way plants are wiser than humans . . .
> at least they try.
> You have to be conscious of your riches
> that are found not so much in the achieving
> as in the trying, the attempt.
> One day the barrier between the attempt
> and the realization will be removed.
> Better to travel than to arrive.
> Seeking is finding.
> Questioning is answering.

In the Mysteries you are stripped and given a garment to cover your loins. You approach the pillars of the Temple and knock three times at the Temple door. Upon entering you are blindfolded and led to a prepared tableau, then hoodwinked—the blindfold is lifted for an instant, then dropped back into place again. All you see is a flash of the tableau, a picture. Because there are no distractions, this highly focused scene becomes impressed on the consciousness, which then begins to work on your psyche.

> Seek and ye shall find.
> Ask and it shall be given.
> Knock and it shall be opened.

These are the three stages in the progression of the discovery of the truth. The seeking is the walking around looking. The asking is a more active stage of involvement. Then there is the knocking at the Temple door. Your body is the temple. Rap on the door with one firm arm that has muscle behind it.

Teachers sit there twiddling their thumbs waiting for the student to ask, really ask . . . not with two arms waving feebly in the air but with one firm arm . . . Will.

[Rinpoche raised his arms to shoulder height, elbows bent, so that his upper and lower arms formed right angles on either side of his body, a gesture of openness and balanced strength.]

This is the Temple.

[Then he crossed his arms in front of his chest in the ancient Egyptian gesture of union and harmony.]

These are the Keys to the Temple.

So . . . when are you going to knock . . . really knock?

19
Working with Hindrances

Q: While meditating yesterday the mind focused on a sound, which then disappeared. Suddenly I experienced a deep fear and was totally locked into it. What can be done when this occurs?

A frozen frame appears if the mind is fixed. This is the mind trying to stabilize itself and is called a "Frozen Ice" type of practice. This should be avoided ... but how? Deepen the calm. This can be done by placing the emphasis more on running, speeding up rather than slowing down before meditating. Then make a distinction between the unborn void and the contents of the mind.

Fear is an enemy. Be alert and treat the fear as an apparition. Dwell on it clearly and loosely. See the fear as a pure dharma, a pure energy. If the apparition disappears, try to repeat the process: consciously bring it up in order to face it.

You can't expect the human being to survive without fear, but you can transform it into calm alertness. In a fear state it is consciousness that flees, not the body. When you are startled your mind will have an alert quality so use the alertness to unfreeze the mind. It is an ego concept to say, *I shouldn't be afraid*. Remove the 'I' from the fear and see only 'fear'.

Mahamudra is not a holy crusade against fear but calmly sees into the nature of fear when it arises. Allow the different mind states to arise spontaneously and then, as this is happening, step back and examine and enter them. The lesson is not to act on the fear but to see that there may be an energy there that can be useful on the path.

In Mahamudra practice there is a stage when you deliberately dredge up all the enemies—fear, sensuality, hatred, restlessness and so on—to see further into their nature. So consciously bring up whatever produces fear in you. See fear and even sickness as energies to use on the path. For example, when you get sick it is usually a sign that you want to get on with real work, so this can become a beneficial time for viewing all the mind states as they arise.

This is not a teaching for babies. It's not just for therapy; it's not just for healing but for the Great Healing. It's a transmutation, not a conquest.

Discipline is needed. Ground yourself in calm and transcend the ego-centeredness. This will bring you to the divine ground of consciousness. On this basis, practise insight: reviewing, not acting out but seeing clearly.

When emotional states arise, catch them as they happen and discipline yourself to ask the question: *What is this?* Then label: *hatred, sensuality, restlessness*—whatever it is. Because you are a human being, you are stuck with wanting love, security, the breast and so forth. But it's not *your* fear; it's not *your* sensuality; it's not *your* problem; it's the whole range of human experience that you can transmute if you are calm. If you push away and pack down the emotion of fear or whatever, it will become a powder keg that will eventually explode. The only way to work with what appears to be unwholesome or evil is to know it, to see it fully. There is a point where the energy flow of fear or hatred has to be raised or transmuted and used for a higher purpose.

There is an aspect of mind that is not swallowed up. Bamboo hates to be confined so it bursts out and grows wherever it can. If you come to a state of mind and fear arises, do not move until it is mastered; let it un-bundle of its own accord. The Buddha said, *I did not move,* when confronted by these enemies. What is meant is consciousness did not move from the ongoing practice of insight.

Keep to the main theme and the dharmas will unfold. You will go from mastery to mastery, from challenge to challenge. This teaching has nothing to do with escapism. All life is escaping. The teaching is purely concerned with seeing what is. See clearly and loosely. The fear, the bundle of doubt, will dissolve in the third eye of its own accord.

After all, they do speak of the mind as a bamboo thicket; it's dense. What are you going to do? Slash your way through with a sword?

S: *The sunlight gets through.*

Yes.

20
Right Effort

Q: *I'm experiencing a great deal of confusion and despair. What can I do?*

You can't deal with neurotic behaviour if you are neurotic, so make the effort toward healthy behaviour.

The Noble Eightfold Path speaks of Right Effort as being fourfold:

> 1. Recognize unwholesomeness as it arises and end it now.
>
> 2. Make effort to prevent it from arising in the future.
>
> 3. Recognize wholesomeness as it arises or is present and affirm, augment and extend it.
>
> 4. Make effort to lay a basis for wholesomeness to arise in the future.

You can either practise Mahamudra or avoid what upsets you. If you know that certain people have an unwholesome affect on you, withdraw from them. This is in the early stage of the teaching; these same people wouldn't be unwholesome to a saint but young people are terribly insecure. It's the old story of lack of know-how; they are vulnerable and insecure because of lack of experience. They try to resolve their problems with their brain and this just leads to despair and confusion. If you realize this is the case, extend the range of your experience.

You can use the skill and means of the teaching: *Come ye out from among them.* The holy life begins with a withdrawal into the desert. Avoid people who make you react. Acquire a peaceful environment and peaceful companions. Clean out the stables, the senses; there's a lot of stuff there that's not integrated. Chuck it out. Shovel out the manure and heap it into a pile.

Calm the body, slow down the breath. This will give you the confidence to meet new experience. Then, from this, lay the emphasis on *Mahaggata* 'the Great Mind, the Great Experience'.

21
Flesh and Bones

Q: In meditation there was the experience of bones on the right side of my body.

There is the experience in the awakening consciousness of the right side of the body pouring forth fire and the left side pouring forth water. Your experience is approaching this state. Hopefully we'll get a full skeleton!

Q: Could you speak a bit more about the 'flesh of the mother' and the 'bones of the father'?

The 'flesh of the mother' is the ground of being. The 'bones of the father' refer to the principle of question making from which the flesh manifests. Blood-milk and flesh-bones are themes of the red and white energies in the body.

There is the koan: *When you return your flesh to your mother and your bones to your father, where are you then?* 'Then' refers to the past, a state before flesh and bones, a state before manifestation and question. Manifestation is forever virgin, and the word *virgin* means 'full, unbroken, complete, un-lost'. The woman is virgin: there is always more growing taking place, more maturing. *Virgin* also means 'maiden'. Christ said to Mary Magdalene, the harlot—promiscuous energy everywhere—*Unless ye become as a man, ye shall not enter the Kingdom of Heaven*. He did not say, *Become a man*. I would add, *Unless ye become as a woman* . . . because you are both. You are always Yab-ing and Yum-ing. All things are mothering and fathering. Eventually you must come to the realization *Before the Universe, I am*.

22
Telepathy

Q: Why does one have telepathic connection with some beings and not with others?

There is a lot of sensing that is not selected to be the centre of the stage. There is another sensing, peripheral consciousness, which is beyond the scope of the senses. It also goes beyond the ego. The greater the awareness the more is received. You could eventually read all beings telepathically by meditation on the heart.

In telepathy, what arises is karmic energy that interlocks with other karmic energy. But all is being received. What you hear depends on your awareness. It has to do with the level of consciousness that is present.

Karma is a field of pulsating energy, not a specific act. Shut up and practise. Transcend the karma by the transcendental moment of the path.

23
Making the Ideal Real

The overall discipline that will bring you to path realization is to become a republic, and a republic is a public thing; it is concrete. You must go from the abstract to the concrete. The whole spiritual trend should be from the ideal to the real, from think-ings to thing-ings, from the bird in the bush to the bird in the hand in daily life.

Many religions are concerned with getting you 'up there', but your work on the spiritual path is not to get to heaven but to bring heaven down to earth.

There are only two teachings in the world: the teaching which respects the material level and sees the divine manifested in it; and the teaching which is oriented toward realization of what is present and making the spiritual more material. This is exemplified in the Ox Herding Pictures. Study them and use them as a guide for realization.

In *Vajrayana*, the Buddha of Integration is *Vajradhara* 'the Diamond-holder'. The *dorje* 'the diamond-tool' held in his right hand is to be used. This manifestation is not static but a present continuous dynamic forming and emptying. In *wongkur* you received the 'initiation' . . . but did you get the realization? Did you make it manifest in your daily life? You must make it public. The realization is not wishy-washy, nor does it have to be a spectacular sign. You must ask yourself: *Has there been a change in the operating consciousness?*

The ground of reality is the ideal, that's why in wongkur the body initiation comes first, as symbolized by the water-filled vase. Water is cohesion, the most bound and yet the loosest of all the five elements. A wongkur is an experience of power. It's given so that you can experience the power and the glory, the ground of reality. Don't worry if the symbols are perhaps too esoteric for your understanding; trust that they have been seeded and will work on you.

You must begin with what is most concrete to you; so first calm the body. Then calm the feelings. Then you can calm the mental formations. This is the natural order of calming the *sankharic* formations of body, speech and mind. You begin with the manifest level, the body, because you want to make the ideal manifest. Make the body the real ideal! You want to loosen the mind. Ah! . . . but where is it? You want to loosen the karma. Ah! . . . but where is it? You want to loosen the body. Aha! . . . there it is . . . the belly!

Practice the four foundations of mindfulness: awareness of body, feeling, states of mind and mental phenomena. Treat them like dogma, as immovable points of awareness. You can't get liberation by wishing; you must tread the path and do the work. The Four Noble Truths contain the essence of the Teaching. If a teaching doesn't speak about suffering and the cessation of suffering, it isn't the teaching. If it doesn't cause the cessation of suffering, it isn't the teaching. The direct way to realization is the practice of mindfulness. In this way, cessation of suffering and illumination are possible. There is work to do.

24
Awareness Is Knowing, Is Mahamudra

To get an idea of the depth meaning of Mahamudra look at the seed syllables that compose the word itself. *Ma* is 'mother'. *Ha* is 'laughter, bliss, happiness'. *Mu* means 'vanishing', and *Dra* is 'foundation, stability'. *Mudra* is 'movement'; things in movement are already on their way to another form. *Maha* means 'great'. So Mahamudra is mothering the joyful disappearance into the ground of being . . .

HA-HA, HA-HA, HO! THE GREAT UNFOLDING!

A being progressing, not ecstatically but simply knowing that suffering has vanished. There is the continuous, ongoing, non-clinging sponsoring of good; more understanding going to greatness. This is the correct unfolding of the flower. Mahamudra is the Great Sign that is no sign. This realization is signless because the being is not clinging.

In Mahamudra you must first be initiated by a qualified lama. There are five stages of the initiation: body, speech, mind, merit and performance or karma unfolding, and you must manifest these five on the path. Be aware of this and register it as information even though you may not be able to make it operative now.

The initiation that is a mind contact with the lama is the introduction to the illuminated clear void. This is a state of non-clinging, abiding where there is non-abiding, a stable flow. We speak of it as the void because there is no clinging to anything in particular. There is freedom that is stable but there is no thing being clung to. There is awareness, knowing of Self-mind and the realization that they are inseparable.

The mind, whilst forming, is also emptying, creating to bring order out of chaos, formings out of the void. The mind, whilst emptying, is also creating: for anything to form there must be emptying. This doesn't negate either emptying or forming. There is order in the process of dissolution. Chaos should be viewed here as potential, the universal potential from which the God-mind is not separate.

> There is your self-mind,
> then Self-mind,
> then God-mind.

> You are Creation and
> Creation is inseparable
> from God-ness.
> It is Mind-selfing.

> The Nature of Mind is to Self,
> to know its own being.
> Only God knows God.
> Only God can un-know God.

Only after this intrinsic awareness of mind is there awareness without content. That doesn't mean there isn't content; it's awareness without boundaries. Neither does it negate contentions. It's re-it, re-it, re-it-ing; a continuous cognizing and awakening to it. This is the ideal making real.

We're changing the entanglements to a knowing of the entanglements in order to elevate mind to a state of non-distinction that incorporates the distinction, and to nonattachment that incorporates the attachment. They are inseparable.

Any distinction you make is already too late; you are a complete entanglement. You are entanglement-ing. There is no subject-object. There is subject-object-making, a happening. We're not saying subject and object don't exist. Change your nouns into verbs to get more and more glimmers. Study the Ox Herding Pictures. Diamond and dung are both carbon.

Practice relaxation and awareness of the daily activities, non-clinging in every moment, void-awareness without content. We must make the path real to you. The Juggler is a good symbol for a Westerner to understand Arising Yoga. It is the introduction into the Great Mind and working with it.

> You have to tread the path because the universe is working.
> You will not be happy apart from working.
> Work is your nature.

> Listen to the story of the awakening mind.
> The teaching is vast and profound.

> Gurus, dwelling in the *Nirmanakaya*,
> just occupy themselves with Universing . . .
> the Grand Play of Illusion.

25
Self-awareness, God-awareness

The essence and pith instruction of the overview of meditation, regardless of the practice you are doing, but especially for Mahamudra, is, *He who can rest his mind in pure Self-awareness without distraction will be able to do anything.*

The mind dwelling easefully, naturally, is in the ongoing presence of God. Pure Self-awareness is God-awareness. The 'will be able to do anything' speaks of the limitless possibilities open to a being in this state. The ongoing awareness of God is not distracted; therefore, it can do anything. There are limitless possibilities because this awareness does not reject this or that aspect. God-awareness encompasses all.

Dukkha 'suffering' is against the flow of the stream. Unwholesome states are consuming much more energy than wholesome states. To practice Mahamudra you must stop discriminating. Abandon *Yes, No*-ing things. Mahamudra 'the Great Going', dwells in non-clinging. Clear awareness is present. It is very simple. It's not so much that you make the effort to drop the habitual thoughts but rather that you see they are limited. *Yes* and *No* discrimination is not bad in itself, but because it is based on partial view it cannot make a good decision with confidence.

If you are concerned with purification, the discrimination has to come from the depths, not from rules or precepts, not even from contact with monks or lamas. Purification has to come from *Lama-mind*, the *Universal-mind*. Trust the depths. In my view, Freud and Jung are ultimately wrong when they refer to the depths as the 'unconscious'. There is the 'collective consciousness' of which you are the 'unconscious'.

> The higher, deeper dharma of planetary or universal evolution is discriminating. Trust it knows the path and will sort you out.

Much of the early work on the path has to do with the practice of dropping the unwholesome and striving to increase the wholesome; but then you have to drop the dropping and the striving. For example, a student brings a rare vase to the teacher who says to him, *Drop it*. After the student does, the teacher again says, *Drop it*; meaning *Now drop the thing you are making of the dropping*.

> The natural state is a flow of automatic perfection beyond accepting and rejecting.

There is liberation through mastery of the negative or unwholesome states, but a lot of energy is spent keeping these states down. For instance, if there is jealousy, you must ask yourself: *Do I keep feeding it by keeping it down?* Don't add fuel to the fire. Because it had a beginning, it will have an end. Let the sin liberate itself.

Keep the continual sounding of God, of the flow, and you will see everything is conditioned and insights will arise. The sounding of God will stop negativity from being fed and positivity from not being seen and understood.

When dealing with problems realize that all phenomena, even your sexual problems, spring from the divine ground, the Great

Awareness. So don't try to get to God-awareness by brooding over or avoiding a problem. Go first to God-awareness and from there to your personal problems, and they will quickly disappear.

In Mahamudra the original mind is pure and has the power to actually purify any unwholesomeness, any problem. Many pitfalls are avoided when you are grounded in this teaching. Instead of saying *I'm trying to heal myself*, let God-nature heal you. So you don't have a problem, even a sexual one, if you trust in God with heart.

The highest therapy is Mahamudra.

The greatest discipline is love.

Get into a state of love.
Wherever you have love
you have a state of union.
Grass is in a state of loving.
Even dying is a state of loving.

Loving is a realization of Self-nature
without beginning, without ending.
There isn't self if there's an 'other'.
You can only have Self when there is no other.

There cannot be living without dying.
In loving there is an intercoursing.
In intercoursing there is the living-dying,
a happening, a changing state.

There is no dharma 'life' by itself.
There is no dharma 'death' by itself.
There is *jati-mara* 'life-death' . . .
an ejaculation, a bursting and an incorporation.

26
Regular Practice and Respect for the Daily Life

The Meditation on Death is a specific examination of karma. Ask: *Why does this energy pass from this state to that state?* It is the nature of consciousness to measure, but in Mahamudra you make the effort to reach the state of *Samma-Samadhi* where *samadhi* and activities become one. *Samma* means 'completely' and *dhi* means 'fixed or stable', so *samadhi* means 'completely fixed'. It is the stable continuum of awareness. *Samadhi* is present in every moment of consciousness; in every moment of consciousness there is activity, a happening, an occurring. Not *your* activity, not *your* *samadhi* but the activity and *samadhi* of the atoms, of all that is occurring.

At first you should stress quiet meditation that calms you or increases tranquillity. Choose any positive wholesome meditation. Then, as an accompanying exercise, apply Mahamudra awareness to daily activities.

Become aware of walking, standing, sitting and lying down. Respect daily life without making a big technique or a big holy out of it. You can't approach meditation with the holies. To live or die more deeply is to respect the daily life. This is a marvelous opportunity. Respect for the ground of happening, respect for the ordinary combined with some kind of regular practice, will lay the basis for lifting you to Mahamudra, to God-mind. If you don't practise these two you cannot gain the path. Unless you respect the daily action you will have false inspiration. Sort out you in the midst of what is happening and see the miracle you are already in. See the logical flowering of the jewel you have in your hand. Anyone who rejects this for that is in fundamental spiritual error. Anyone who discriminates is split, sick. The path is union, presence.

Begin with the miracles of this world and eventually this will unfold into other dharmas. Don't reverse it; avoid dharmas of the inner plane that may terrify you if you are not grounded.

The path is union, presence. This must be stressed. Have faith. Begin with what you already have, the miracle of this world. Let it unfold and it will incorporate all dharma. On these pebbles the deities and the demons will become HO HUM!

There is the great temptation to say: *If only I had this* . . . Put this sin down. Appreciate what is happening and practise meditation as if it were something ordinary. You are already in the garden; you have only to eat of the fruit.

I don't care how many centuries of error takes place, whether it is the misinterpretation of Christ's teaching or the planet going up in smoke, this path is the most logical.

> A creature should begin with its creature-ness,
> its daily activities,
> not its acquisition of spiritual 'goodies'
> or a 'spiritual' life.
> Know thyself.
> Then you will find treasures.
> As soon as you begin the work
> you are already on the path.

Develop equilibrium, relaxation and naturalness of body, speech and mind. Balance the body—the cells, the contents of the body—by loosening or shaking it to make it flexible. Balance the mouth—speech, the energy flows—by slowing down the breathing or allowing it to slow down by itself. This will lead to the sorting out of the energy, the karmic formations. Balance the mind by getting rid of concepts; drop rigidity of mind and naturalness will come into play.

A cell is an energy exchange and a knowing. Every cell has consciousness. You are a whole society, a whole force field of types and strata of energies: consciousness engaged in infinite formings and dissolutions, communicating and contributing to a shifting, molding, knowing.

Once there is balance and this knowing, you will attain the experience of energy breath. It's not just you breathing but atoms and cells breathing. There is Breathing! This is the overview that sees breathing as an exchange of energies. We are constantly exchanging energies of different molecular forms.

Abandon rigidity of body, speech and mind. Your fixed views make you insecure. Let them go, say, *I don't know*. Open your mind to new ideas and you will have greater ideas and greater security. All this will produce a physical ease. Then body, speech and mind will naturally correlate and integration will take place.

It is not compassionate to put yourself through a fantastic effort. All that suffering of St. Theresa is just not necessary. Let the effortless effort of consciousness unfold. Let it speed up or slow down of its own accord.

**Abandon *your* exercise!
The whole universe is exercising!**

The highest dharma is communication. Only by communication can forms be made. Wherever you have communication you have forms. Wherever you have forms you have communication, body, speech and mind OM AH HUM-ing. They're conjoined and happening at the same time: the *Dharmakaya*, *Sambhogakaya* and *Nirmanakaya*, the instantaneous divine ground. The jewel is flowering; the energy is unfolding.

Every cell sparkles. These are bombardments, like knocking out pins, discharging accumulated energies. These discharges are necessary for the new formings to come into being. Hopefully this energy exchange will incorporate into another karma that is helpful to the unfolding of your being. This has a lot to do with energy travelling up and down the spine. Explosions in the head are okay . . . but be careful, there might be a problem if the energy goes out the third eye. The explosions and knocks are a sign that the energy has not been smoothed out. So this must sort itself out until it comes to a smooth flow. Have a positive view of this. Alleviate the explosions if they're too violent by more contact with daily life, with naturalness. Be with the earth and drop your concept of meditation!

Tennyson said, *If I could understand this little flower growing in a crannied wall I would know it all*. In the mystical life there is a point where you have to stop working strenuously and see the flower, smell the flower. Put down your burden, return to Eden and walk with the Lord in the Garden.

27
Five Similes of Mahamudra

[In the following discourse Rinpoche frequently referred to various passages in The Teaching of Tibetan Yoga, *translated and annotated by Garma C. C. Chang. New Hyde Park, New York, University Press, 1963.]*

The three essentials in the practice of Mahamudra are equilibrium, relaxation and naturalness. Equilibrium refers to the balancing of the body, energy and mind. Relaxation rests in loosening the mind and the *sankharic* formations; letting go of concepts, stripping the mind of thoughts and ideas and transcending verbalization. Naturalness means living according to nature, dwelling without taking or leaving anything.

Let the senses and the mind stop and flow by themselves without restricting or promoting them. If you promote or deny something it's planned and therefore not spontaneous, it's affected behaviour. One needs no effort to be natural and completely spontaneous. Spontaneity in a clear, aware, natural state means going with the flow and letting things sort themselves out. You will know by the light the degree to which you are spontaneous. Golden or saffron light is present in this state.

Obviously there is a planning going on, this is the only way to live—with your feet on the ground—but it's not necessarily *you* planning.

The teaching is testable. Trust in dharma; it is affirming. You will know if there is an improvement. In a sense, for very little effort you get a great reward.

There are five similes by which you may know if the practice is proceeding correctly. It sounds poetic but these descriptive qualities of mind are literal.

> 1. *The mind is like a vast sphere of infinite space in all directions. You sense it rather than see it.* This is integration.

> 2. *Awareness is omnipresent of every moment of consciousness.* This is recollectedness or knowing. You're aware of what is taking place and not lost in fantasy. It's seeing the whole story like seeing all the geography of the earth, its mountains, valleys, deserts and fields. The awareness is present in all the experiences: Eros and Logos, wet and dry, cold and warm. The earth represents the round and non-discriminate geography of the mind.

> 3. *The mind is steady as a mountain.* Like a triangle or pyramid, it has a steady broad base with its tip or peak in space. This represents the steady upward ascent, constant development and a sensing of the vast possibilities. Like a mountain it has its roots in the earth, and its top, the peak, is in the vast emptiness of space. In Japan they meditate on an empty teacup, then pour the tea into it and taste it—the mind can be filled with anything.

4. *Self-realizing awareness.* This is finding the key in your being that is illuminating. Clearness of mind is the illumination, not the different lights you see in meditation. Self-realizing awareness is clear and bright like a lamp on a windless night. The spreading light shows up the possibilities of the diamond-mind. Illumination must shine; there is an ongoing increase of knowing. The clay butter lamps on Tibetan shrines represent the inner lights and chakras. There is an increase in awareness; things that were in the dark before are now known, Self-realizing in the presence of God. This is the awakening factor of mind.

5. *Pure consciousness, crystal clear.* There is a feeling of purity. The emphasis is on crystal, which reflects everything. It is clear and empty of discriminating thoughts.

These five qualities: infinite space, awareness omnipresent, steadiness, the awakening factor of mind and purity, may be accompanied by physical experiences and/or archetypal symbols. For instance, you may feel you are in boundless space or experience yourself as a sphere of space. You may experience yourself being raised to heaven or to a point, or sinking into the bowels of the earth, or becoming a crystal.

If you recognize that one of the five factors is present and if you don't cling to that one, all the factors may come together for the experience of *Samma-Sambuddha*. These experiences come into the daily life as an affirmation of your practice. It's not going to be some great big bang, although there are definitive experiences called 'seals'. The experiences will be an affirmation of your daily life.

Mahamudra experience has also been described thus:

> *Like a cloudless sky, the sphere is broad*
> *and free from obstruction.*
> *Like a wave-less ocean, the mind is steady*
> *without discriminating thoughts.*
> *Like a lamp on a windless night,*
> *the consciousness is clear, bright, and stable.*

Walk with awareness from where you are. See the totality around you in all directions.

In the beginning you have waves and ripples, discriminating thoughts; the mind is tumbling like a waterfall and arbitrary, then becomes a stream with many stops-and-goes. Gradually the debris floats by. You may think at first that this is the nature of mind, but then it slows, the sun and moon merge into one steadiness: *Like a lamp on a windless night . . .* Why not on a windless day? The lamp is unbounded consciousness, which is clear, bright and stable. It is not a flickering light with shadows still there, concerned with the appearances of reality. The night represents the apparent limits of consciousness; but Self-realizing awareness is a lamp on a windless *day*—unbounded consciousness.

Keep the body loose and gentle; trust the balancing of the universal dharma. Treat all you encounter as the unborn void. To identify everything with the unborn void is to see the infinite possibilities around you. There is no clinging to anything in particular. *Put your cares in Jesus.* When there is trust in God everything you meet liberates itself. To keep the body loose and gentle does not mean abandoning activity but doing it in a smooth, relaxed way. Don't linger. Why have a debate? Centre your consciousness and turn the wheel. Don't make statements. Make questions. This is Bright Awareness.

By your faith ye shall know, by your works ye shall be known. Faith is not belief in this or that, it is an operative faith that has to give rise to works. Not *My will be done*, but *Thy will be done*. Become more relaxed, pick up existence and experience it. This will bring you immediate fruits, which lead you on to Buddha Awareness.

28
Symbolism

Q: I've been experiencing different colours in meditation, also symbols: a dog, a triangle. What approach can I take in interpreting these?

Symbolism follows certain laws. First you have the symbol that is based on the collective experience of consciousness, often referred to as the collective unconscious. Secondly, you have the symbol that is based on the personal conditioning of the individual who is experiencing the symbol. The teacher can indicate the meaning of a symbol on the collective level, and although he can also indicate a direction for you to pursue in interpreting the symbol on a personal level, he can't liberate you from the personal conditioning. Only you can liberate that. However, from your dialogue with the teacher you will be able to work out the personal meaning for your liberation.

In general, blue symbolizes tranquillity; white, purity; yellow, spontaneity; and brown, physical ease. Red, a comparative rarity in nature, represents will. It's also a colour that is used to indicate communication, as, for example, on the Canada Post Office box. A dog is a companion of man as the body is the companion of the spirit. An upward pointed triangle is a symbol of aspiration.

Your approach to every symbol should cover the two levels of interpretation: the universal or physiological level—the story of humanity's unfoldment—and the personal or psychological level, for this you must be aware of the dimension of personal association.

In dialogue, the teacher can't be too premature in describing the personal level because the student may not be ready to understand it fully.

29
Anicca, Dukkha, Anatta

There are three ways in which all phenomena are perceived. In any experience when the emphasis is on quickness, it's insight into the nature of *anicca* 'impermanence'. If the emphasis is on heaviness, it's insight into the nature of *dukkha* 'suffering'. If the emphasis is on lightness, it's insight into the nature of *anatta* 'easeful insubstantiality'.

For instance, in one of the early stages of *Vipassana* one may experience a falling star. This is insight into *anicca*. In the experience of being raised to heaven and plunged to earth there's just arising and cessation; that's a direct seeing . . . but how? Was it seen as *anicca*, *dukkha* or *anatta*?

These dharmas must be seen in their pristine purity. If there's *anicca*, there's just *anicca*; if there's *dukkha*, there's just *dukkha*; if there's *anatta*, there's just *anatta*. In any experience you must notice which of the three characteristics is predominant: quickness, heaviness or lightness.

30
The Only Work You Have

It is appropriate in the beginning of the work to dangle the carrot before the student; but then the teacher has the responsibility to teach that the universe is a charnel ground. You are already a corpse burning. We are all grist for the mill, the burial place. The meditation on death teaches the one sure thing, that you will die. Death is sure; life is uncertainty. If you incorporate this fact into your life you will use your energies correctly and wisely.

Once you know you are burning you will realize the only work you have is to awaken. And the only way to awaken is to love fully and to know fully. And the only way to love fully and to know fully is to be aware.

If you don't know your own origination or cessation, how can you help others? How can you save others? You have not got time to concern yourself with other people's problems at this stage. Use your eyes, use your ears, patiently practise awareness.

31
Through the Senses—
The Transcendental

[During the retreat, Rinpoche occasionally would bring a box containing small bottles of perfume essences for us to explore, a different one or two each time.]

Scent is the most elaborate and subtle of your senses. You never really taste anything without the sense of smell. A good example of this is when you have a cold: you don't taste the food you are eating because your sense of smell is impaired. The ranges of bitter to sweet tastes are really smells that originate from the release of certain enzymes and chemicals in the body.

The sense of smell is cognized in the cells of the olfactory lobes, which developed in ancient times when predators were mostly on the ground. Food then, was found by sound and smell; sight was too late, especially in the jungle. For instance, a dog being earth-centered, needs sound and smell for survival. There were fewer predators above the ground so eventually our ancestral primates took to the trees for safety. There was also a more abundant supply of food there. The abundance of food may have led to playing with it and a resultant bonk on the head could have inspired the first weapon. The first aggressions were undoubtedly about food and sex.

Later, when primates moved to the open plains, sight rather than smell became the most important sense for survival. However, because smell developed in the oldest part of the brain, it is probably the strongest of the senses. In many mental illnesses the sense of smell can be overwhelming: for instance, a smell in the mouth can pervade a room.

Because the sense of smell goes back to the ancient mind, scent is one of the clues on the mystical path. Putrescence can be transmuted into ambrosial delights by the experience of the transcendental. You should explore perfume because you have the obligation to transcend what you are, to transmute into sweetness, to go to the higher *per - fume!*

Consciously use your sense of smell and develop sensitivity to odours. If you explore all the senses you will loosen, expand and sharpen them. Beings are dead if they don't make the conscious effort to explore the senses.

Heaven and earth declare the glory of God. God won't come to you unless you go to God. You can't get it cerebrally; it's not in the books. Go to meet the senses and they will come to you. You must consciously expand and loosen them to attain *Mahaggata* 'Great-going'.

How can the transcendental be made real to you? When you are involved in awareness of sensing, the transcendental raises the question: *There must be an origin.*

If you find a sense of wonder in the universe, how much more wonderful the creator!

A being is a pendulum swinging from passivity to activity, from extroversion to introversion, from intellect to feeling, from sensing to intuition. The pendulum swings are wider when there is unbalanced exploration. The swings are an attempt to bring about balance because balance is the only way to happiness. Shorten the pendulum swings by being aware. If you're passive, be aware of passivity.

There are extroverted and introverted aspects of each of the four functions of the psyche: sensing, feeling, thinking and intuition. For example, the mechanic expresses the extroverted sensing function; the artist, the introverted sensing function. Explore each of the four functions and the pools of experience will integrate and awareness will lead you from perpetual motion to a still point of balance.

The young psyche is prone to drastic and extreme solutions. Most people would intuit the transcendental through the integration of the senses; even a mere infant knows this. The danger is in the non-struggle, in the hopelessness that ends up in anti-spiritualism or in spiritual disorientation.

For the path to be lived properly you need your senses functioning finely and fully. They can't if they are drugged. People take drugs because they are out of contact with their being. They don't trust their own organism and by taking drugs they are making a statement of failure. When the feeling of ineffectiveness arises, instead of taking a tranquillizer or a stimulant, why not just consciously say: *I can't do it*.

The fifth precept of Buddhism is: *I undertake to train myself to refrain from taking intoxicants that cloud the mind and cause heedlessness*. The Teaching is down on drugs unless it leads to awareness and clarity. Senseless indulgence is definitely out. To be free one must be clear.

The use of drugs—which predominates in different societies in certain cycles on the planet—is born from spiritual infancy. It is an oral regression arising from a negative view of the self. Drugs satisfy the passive-femininity drive. Why not just realize you are dependent on the breast? Simply abandon your ego and do what you want and need to, but do it consciously. Become as little children and play in the fields of the Lord. Be feminine, be dependent. If you don't realize your dependence you won't realize your independence.

S: In watching arising and passing away through the senses there was the experience 'I' didn't know what 'it'—this whole organism—was doing. I feel like an idiot!

Very good: *I - Dio* 'with God'.

32
Fantasy

Q: Does fantasy have any place in the Teaching?

Fantasy is simply a mind creation and dissolution. Arising Yoga uses fantasy as a creative force to help unfold a being. The major element of mental illness starts off with fantasy. It is a retreat from reality, from what is present because the love and attention needed is missing. You dream about the candy you did not get. All fantasy is wish fulfillment. It is a statement that the ongoing is not satisfactory. When the present becomes boring you go back to the past or dwell on what you're going to do in the future. On the interpersonal plane, there is sexual fantasy. All attainments—buildings, art, science and so on—are based on dissatisfaction. Most beings spend eighty to ninety percent of their time in fantasy, maybe more.

How unreal are you? This is the first question you must ask yourself. In mental illness, the major sign is the repetitive and morbid fantasy that feeds the ego. Find out how much of your time is spent in fantasy.

In a pure state of mind, if you actually believe something firmly you can create it and change the course of reality. Be more or less there in the fields first, then you can idealize it. In *Vajrayana* you consciously build enlightened formations in the mind and then dissolve them. Through this process you can change the nature of reality.

Your view of yourself as Bodhisattva or Jesus is fantasy. If you create the illusion constantly and consciously, you may ultimately become it. You have to see how impossible it is so that the fantasy can be transcended and become an embodied truth. It can't do that unless fantasy is in accord with reality. Being limited and partial, you are in *maya* 'illusion'. But you can work with it through Arising Yoga. Because there is dissolution of the creation, letting go, you are not caught in it. Mandala making is a fantasy creation. St. Francis had a fantasy; he spent time and effort on it and built a church, a reality.

> Total commitment or involvement in awakening
> will produce the fruit.
> You will become the translucent sphere.
> You will become ready to receive the waters.
> But you spend your time piddling around in fantasy.
> Well, the Teaching wipes you out.
> You're a limited being.
> Therefore, you have only a reflection of reality.
> That's not bamboo you see,
> you project your fantasy onto it.

Why are we fantasy making? . . . To lead us somewhere. It is a way of searching, a way to see more possibilities. In the Teaching there are certain ranges of consciousness—when *maya* is seen as *Maya*—that are able to use fantasy for liberation. You can use it if you know what you're doing. For example, in sexual fantasy you can awaken the principle of *Dorje Phagmo,* or Marilyn Monroe for that matter; you can awaken the *Demchog* principle or Clark Gable. The main difference between the Hollywood fantasy and the *Vajrayana* deities is that the latter hold powerful tools in their hands that are used for liberation.

Fantasizing is a basic human dharma. You worrying about fantasizing is an ego-projection. Get in touch with and become the aspect or focus of the fantasy and use it for transmutation. The whole finite universe fantasizes because one atom can't know all other atoms. Grass gets by on fantasy, on partial views. But you do have to get to the God view, which is something else. It is the total view that knows all the fantasies.

The whole universe is Maya maya-ing!

33
Resting on Fact

The theme of the meditation is more important in the early stages of the practice than the technique. Death is a vast subject, its theme starts crudely but gradually you learn to refine it until it becomes subtle. When you are ready, technique will help you move in for the kill . . . of the ego.

If you were to have the certainty or full realization of death you would automatically be liberated. You would experience joy, spontaneity and more energy.

If you were in touch with the earth you would experience the union of the senses; you would have a bubbling flow because any healthy exploration of the senses and the intellect immediately brings joy and spontaneity. Unfortunately, you are a copier, it's not your discovery so there's no joy. Most of what passes for intellect is an ego affectation. Every being has an obligation to make a new idea, to stimulate, to bring forth from the intellect a gift to the universe. Don't bury your talent, develop it.

The greatest cross I bear is boring students. You have an obligation to stimulate the teacher. You can feel the chains of beings that are in the bondage of the pseudo-intellect. The pure intellect itself has a feeling of effervescence, spontaneity, quickness and facility.

When Jesus said you must die to the world he meant you must die to the worldly conditioning, the partial views. These fall away with the realization of death and you are able to perceive things as they really are.

Through sensing, feeling, thinking and intuiting and their integration, you become free. I assure you, the song of life will be beautiful once you experience a true, deep realization of death. Until then, life is subject to being cut off in midstream. Only *Yamantaka* 'Destroyer of the Lord of Death' will cut through *samsara*. Your ego emotions about death will not do anything; the only thing that will is the absolute resting on fact. Sad or happy about death, once it becomes a real fact there is an enormous difference in the song of life. All the responses on many levels change, the realizations are immediate.

**All your responses to life are the ego of today . . .
as if the former ego of the last lifetime has never been.
You must transcend the ego.**

Death is the certainty,
life the uncertainty, the spontaneity.
Life must be lived uncertainly.
Let the potential way of living become the actual.
It is *dukkha* to try to make the impermanence of life permanent.
Perceive that all things that have a beginning have an end.
When you realize impermanence, *dukkha* becomes *sukha*.

All is perpetually originating,
without beginning, without ending.
You are constantly changing
whether you know it or not.
All you need is *prajna* 'right view'.
Nothing has to be altered.
Samsara and *nirvana* are one.
Lighten your burden.
Anatta 'un-self' you.
In that sense there is no ego.
There is no 'you'.
There is only mutation.

People who are not aware of
the process of mutation
are in a living death.
Their intellectual plane is dead.
Their discovery plane is dead.
They're getting senile.
You should ask:
What is it in my being
that is producing the non-seeing?
You must make the effort to
become free of non-seeing.
You must even make the effort to
get away from the teacher's feet.

It's good to take the scrolls out of the tabernacle
and have a look at them.

If my realization is true,
others' erroneous views cannot alter that.

Glossary

Pali (P), Sanskrit (S), Tibetan (T)

Abhidhamma (P): [*abhi* 'high', *dhamma* 'law, truth or teaching'] the third of the three main divisions constituting the Pali Canon, the scriptures of Theravada Buddhism. Its subject matter consists entirely of the analysis of mind and matter, their causes and conditionality.

Anatta (P): not-self, no permanent identity, no abiding self or substance.

Anicca (P): not permanent; all conditioned things are changing, in flux.

Arising Yoga: a meditation practice involving visualization and mantra leading to insight into the arising and dissolution of form.

Aryan, Arya (S): the ruling clan in Northern India at the time of the Buddha, hence *ariya* 'noble, distinguished, of high birth, right, good, ideal'.

Asubha (P): impurity, that which is not beautiful. The Asubha Meditations consist of the Cemetery Contemplations (stages of decomposition of a corpse) and the Meditation on the Thirty-Two Parts of the Body, both of which are antidotes against the hindrance of sense-desire.

Bija (S): seed, seed syllable, used as a metaphor for the origin or cause of things. Mystical mantras are composed of pure sound seed syllables.

Bodhisattva (S): enlightenment being, one who has vowed to attain complete awakening in order to benefit all sentient beings. A specialized use of the term describes one who has attained any of the Ten Stages of a Bodhisattva.

Buddha-Dharma (S) *Buddha-Dhamma* (P): the laws, science and teachings of enlightenment as rediscovered and then expounded by the Buddha.

Cakra (P): wheel; centre; eye; energy nexus within the subtle energy body.

Chenrezi (T): The Great Bodhisattva, embodiment of compassion of all the Buddha's dedicated to alleviating the suffering of beings and bringing them to enlightenment.

Demchog (T): a principal *yidam* 'tutelary deity' in Tibetan Schools of Buddhism. Embodiment of Supreme Bliss and Emptiness, his main attribute is the ability to transform the most unpromising worldly situations instantly into the power of insight.

Dharma (S) *Dhamma* (P): the bearer, constitution or nature of a thing, norm, law, doctrine, justice, righteousness, quality, thing, object of mind and phenomenon; the science and teaching of the laws of enlightenment; the term used for phenomena that may be of the past, present or future, material or mental, conditioned or not, real or imaginary.

Dharmakaya (S): the ultimate or universal body of an Enlightened One (Buddha) that is beyond all forms, attributes and limits.

Dorje (T) *Vajra* (S): a ritual object symbolizing the indestructible properties of a diamond and irresistible force of a thunderbolt and representing firmness of spirit and the supreme power of compassionate skill and means.

Dorje Phagmo (T): one of the central *yidams* 'tutelary deities' of the Kagyu School of Tibetan Buddhism, she embodies the active cutting through of all obstacles on the path and the complete utilization of energy for enlightenment.

Dukkha (P): contention, anguish, that which is hard to bear, hard to endure, often translated as 'suffering' but refers more widely to the unsatisfactory and impermanent nature of all conditioned phenomena.

Dukkha-cariya (P): an extreme form of asceticism practiced by Gautama before he attained enlightenment and Buddhahood.

Four Noble Truths: The briefest synthesis of the entire Teaching: The Truth of *Dukkha* 'Suffering', The Truth of the Origin of Suffering, The Truth of the Cessation of Suffering and The Truth of the Eightfold Path leading to the Cessation of Suffering.

Guru (S): one who is unshakable, one who has heard the divine word, a spiritual teacher.

Guru Rinpoche (T): the great teacher-saint, founder of Buddhism in Tibet in the 8th century, also known as *Padmasambhava*.

Janus: in Roman mythology, the god of gates, doors, doorways, depicted as having two faces or heads facing in opposite directions simultaneously, the new and the old.

Jati (P): birth. [Note: during this retreat Rinpoche sometimes used *jati* synonymously with the Pali word *jivita* 'life'. Ed.]

Jhana (P): absorption achieved through the attainment of full concentration of mind on a mental or physical object during which there is a complete, though temporary, suspension of five-fold sense activity and of the five hindrances (*nivarana*).

Karma (S) *Kamma* (P): action or activity denoting the wholesome and unwholesome volitions and their concomitant mental factors, causing rebirth and shaping the future events of beings. These karmic volitions become manifest as wholesome or unwholesome actions by body, speech and mind.

Kasina (P): an external device used as a focus to develop concentration of mind through the four fine-material absorptions (*rupa-jhana*). [The Ten Kasina Meditations are listed on page 1. Ed.]

Kundalini (S): coiled; the evolutionary energy in man; serpent-power; innate energy coiled up at the root of the spinal column which can be activated and utilized by means of Yoga techniques for physical, emotional, mental and spiritual healing.

Mahamudra (S): [*maha* 'great', *mudra* 'gesture, sign, seal'] great sign or great seal; an insight practice based primarily on non-clinging awareness and the direct seeing of the essential unqualified emptiness of all phenomena.

Mahayana (S): lit. Great Vehicle. One of the three levels of Buddhism which emphasizes the emptiness of all phenomena, great compassion for all beings and realization of universal Buddha-Nature.

Mandala (S): a spiritual and ritual symbol representing an enlightened form or the universe; any diagram, chart or geometric pattern that represents the cosmos metaphysically or symbolically; an object constructed for the development of concentration, integration and expansion of mind; a term used to indicate the totality of activity and experience at any given moment.

Manodvara (P): [*mano* 'mind', *dvara* 'door'] the mind-door through which mental objects are perceived.

Mantra (S): [*mano* 'mind', *tra* 'to fix'] sacred utterance, numinous sound or a syllable, word, or group of syllables or words used to transcend dualistic thought and to attain an enlightened state and/or characteristic(s).

Maya (P/S): illusion, the cosmic illusion of duality, appearance, as opposed to reality.

Milarepa: (1052-1135 BCE), the great poet-saint of Tibet who taught through his mystic songs of enlightened realization.

Mon (P): an ethnic group from Burma, the Mon were responsible for the spread of Buddhism in Indochina. Geographically associated with Milarepa, their land was close to that part of Tibet where he lived.

Namarupa (P): [*nama* 'name', hence 'mind'; *rupa* 'form or matter'] mind and matter, mentality and corporeality.

Nibbana (P) *Nirvana* (S): that dharma which remains after complete craving has been eradicated; the emancipation from all sorrows; extinction of all roots of unwholesomeness (greed, hatred and delusion): transcendent and singularly ineffable liberation.

Nirmanakaya (S): the dimension of ceaseless manifestation; the physical body of an enlightened being.

Noble Eightfold Path: the last of the Four Noble Truths, i.e. the Path to the Cessation of Suffering, namely:

1. Right View	III. Wisdom
2. Right Thought	
3. Right Speech	I. Morality
4. Right Bodily Action	
5. Right Livelihood	
6. Right Effort	II. Concentration
7. Right Mindfulness	
8. Right Concentration	

In actual practice, the path begins with cultivating moral training (links 3-5), then mental training (links 6-8), and then wisdom (links 1-2).

Ox Herding Pictures: a series of short poems and accompanying pictures used in the Zen tradition to illustrate a practitioner's stages of progression towards the purification of the mind and enlightenment, as well as his or her subsequent return into the world while acting with wisdom.

Pancadvara (P): [*panca* 'five', *dvara* 'door, gate'] the five sense-doors through which objects of the five senses are perceived.

Path Experience: the experience of the transcendental; the first of four definite stages of realization on the path to Buddhahood (commonly referred to in Pali as *Sotappanna* 'Stream-Winner') in which the first three fetters are removed: belief in a permanent self, skeptical doubt and attachment to rules and rituals.

Piti (P): physical bliss, joy, zest, interest.

Prajna (S): wisdom; transcendental wisdom that is non-dual and non-discriminative.

Prana (S) *pana* (P): air, breath, energy, vital force, spirit, sometimes refers to energy or air currents in the body.

Pranayama (S): a breath control exercise usually practiced in conjunction with various body postures, as in Yoga, for example.

Qabbalah: (also spelled *Kabalah*) refers to either of two sets of esoteric teachings, the Hermetic and the Hebraic, regarding the relationship between the eternal and mysterious creator and the mortal and finite universe. Each includes the use of symbols and systems, such as The Tree of Life, to interpret these teachings as a path to intuitive realization.

Samadhi (P): concentration, one-pointedness of mind. Concentration, though often weak, is one of the seven mental factors common to all states of consciousness.

Samana (P): wanderer, recluse following the discipline of the religious life.

Samatha (P): any meditation leading to calm and tranquillity.

Sambhogakaya (S): the energy/bliss body, body of enjoyment, energy field or play of an enlightened being.

Samma-Ditthi (P): Right or Total View, the complete understanding and realization of the Four Noble Truths.

Samma-Samadhi (P): Right or Complete Concentration, as the last link of the Eightfold Path, it is defined as the four meditative absorptions (*Jhana*). In a wider sense it is associated with all karmic wholesome states of consciousness.

Samma-Sambuddha (P): a completely enlightened, fully manifested Buddha.

Samsara (P) round of rebirth, lit. perpetual wandering; the unbroken chain of blind, habitual patterns of body, speech and mind activity.

Sankhara (P): formation; wholesome or unwholesome volitional activity; the prior conditioning or expectation present in any event thus perpetuating habitual patterning.

Sixteen Stages of Insight: sixteen stages of direct seeing or direct knowledge into the nature of mind and matter comprising the progression of the path of liberation.

Skandhas (S) *Khandhas* (P): aggregates or heaps. Specifically refers to five aspects of all physical and mental phenomena of existence: form or matter, feeling or sensation, perception, mental or volitional formations and consciousness.

Sukha (P): [*su* 'good, happy'; *kha* 'formation, forming, space'] a pleasant, wholesome mental formation; happiness, all-rounded satisfaction or ease.

Tanha (P): lit. thirst, craving; the chief root of suffering and the ever continuing cycle of rebirths.

Tantra (S): lit. thread; *Vajrayana* teachings outlining mystic practices leading directly to enlightenment.

Tara (S): the compassionate female embodiment of enlightenment usually portrayed in green or white form, protector and remover of all obstacles on the path.

Tarot: a Western tradition of esoteric knowledge whose picture-symbols embody universal principals that focus on individual spiritual progress through initiation, study of philosophy and cosmic laws and their practical application.

Upekkha (P): equanimity free of attachment and aversion, mental balance, at-one-ment.

Vajradhara (S): the Primordial Buddha, holder of the diamond state of consciousness, Root Guru of the Kagyu School.

Vajrasattva (S): diamond-being, the enlightened manifestation of utter purity dwelling in the complete union of wisdom and the skill-in-means to awaken it in others. In the Tibetan teaching, *Vajrasattva* is perhaps the most important practice to complete as it purifies the auric body, thus cleansing karmic bonds.

Vajrayana (S): diamond-vehicle, the instantaneous, direct path of awakening transcending all duality. The third vehicle of Buddhism, it is distinguished by its variety of practices to bring beings quickly to liberation.

Vipassana (P): insight, the intuitive seeing of the truth of the impermanent, suffering and impersonal or insubstantial nature of all physical and mental phenomena of existence, i.e. *anicca, dukkha* and *anatta*.

Wongkur (T): empowerment; an initiation in which a specific enlightened mind-energy-body state is invoked by the Lama and transmitted to those present.

Yab-Yum (S): the male-female aspect of divinity in union personifying the transcendence of all dualities; the oneness free from polarity.

Yamantaka (S): a tantric deity, the wrathful form of *Manjusri*, Bodhisattva of Discriminating Wisdom.

Publications of Namgyal Rinpoche's Discourses

BOOKS

A Body of Truth, Empowering through Active Imagination and Creative Visualization, Edited by Rab Wilkie, Leslie Hamson and Karma Chime Wongmo, Kinmount, Ontario, Bodhi Publishing, 1997.

Body, Speech & Mind, a manual for human development, Namgyal Rinpoche, Edited by Cecilie Kwiat, Kinmount, Ontario, Bodhi Publishing, Second Edition, 2004.

Glimmerings of the Mystical Life, Namgyal Rinpoche, Compiled by Margaret Morris, Kinmount, Ontario, Bodhi Publishing, Second Edition, 2002.

Paleochora Discourses, Part I, *Exploring the Language of Liberation,* Part II, *Healing, Faith and Karma,* Namgyal Rinpoche, Kinmount, Ontario, Bodhi Publishing, 2009.

Right Livelihood and Other Foundations of Enlightenment, Namgyal Rinpoche, Kinmount, Ontario, Bodhi Publishing, 2008.

Suchness, the Diamond State of Realization, Teachings on the Diamond Sutra, Namgyal Rinpoche, Edited by Karma Chime Wongmo, Kinmount, Ontario, Bodhi Publishing, 2006.

The Breath of Awakening, A Guide to Liberation Through Ānāpānasati, Mindfulness of Breathing, Namgyal Rinpoche, Edited by Karma Chime Wongmo, Kinmount, Ontario, Bodhi Publishing, 1992, Second Edition 2019.

The Path of Victory, Discourses on the Paramita, Namgyal Rinpoche, Edited by Sonam Senge, Boise, Idaho, The Open Path Publishing, 1982; Kinmount, Ontario, Bodhi Publishing, Fourth Printing, 2002.

The Song of Awakening, A Guide to Liberation through Maranussati *'Mindfulness of Death',* Namgyal Rinpoche, Edited by Karma Chime Wongmo, First Edition, Boise, Idaho, The Open Path Publishing, 1979. Second Edition, Peterborough, Ontario, Bodhi Publishing, 2021.

Unfolding Through Art, Namgyal Rinpoche, Edited by Karma Chime Wongmo, Boise Idaho, The Open Path Publishing, 1982. Property of Bodhi Publishing.

The Womb, Karma and Transcendence, A Journey towards Liberation, Namgyal Rinpoche, Edited by Karma Chime Wongmo, Kinmount, Ontario, Bodhi Publishing, 1996.

The Womb of Form, Pith Instructions in The Six Yogas of Naropa, Namgyal Rinpoche, Kinmount, Ontario, Bodhi Publishing, 1998.

BOOKLETS

Holistic Clearing Meditation, An Antiparalytic Meditation for Human Liberation, Namgyal Rinpoche, Kinmount, Ontario, Bodhi Publishing, Revised 1989.

The Dome of Heaven, Awakening, Namgyal Rinpoche, Kinmount, Ontario, Bodhi Publishing.

The Meditation on Peace, Namgyal Rinpoche, Edited by Karma Chime Wongmo, Kinmount, Ontario, Bodhi Publishing, 1986.

MP3 AUDIO DISCOURSES

Suchness, the Diamond State of Realization, Teachings on the Diamond Sutra, Namgyal Rinpoche, Edited by Karma Chime Wongmo and Jeff Riches, Kinmount, Ontario, Bodhi Publishing, 2006. (Previously available as an Audio Set of 6 CDs, these discourses are now available as MP3s on our website at www.bodhipublishing.org)

BOOKS BY OTHER AUTHORS

Altruism, Contemplations for the Scientific Age, Karma Sonam Senge, Boise, Idaho, The Open Path Publishing, 1986. Property of Bodhi Publishing.

Why Meditate? A Heart Song of Vast Release, Mark Webber, Kinmount, Ontario, Bodhi Publishing, 2000, Second Printing 2019.

TO ORDER OUR PUBLICATIONS,
please visit our website at www.bodhipublishing.org

BODHI PUBLISHING is a registered non-profit, charitable organization dedicated to publishing books on universal awakening as transmitted by Namgyal Rinpoche for the benefit of all beings. Our vision is to share these teachings with those who are interested in and committed to developing awareness, compassion and wisdom in their daily lives. In doing so we strive to make each publication a work of high quality craftsmanship.

Our editions vary in size and form. Aside from printing and binding, the majority of all work that goes into creating a book—transcribing, editing, design, lay-out and art—is done by volunteers who, in the spirit of generosity, contribute their skills, energy and time.

Donations to publish and reprint Rinpoche's discourses are much appreciated. If you would like to make a donation, please make it payable to BODHI PUBLISHING and send it to our mailing address. Donors will receive a receipt for income tax purposes.

www.ingramcontent.com/pod-product-compliance
Lightning Source LLC
Chambersburg PA
CBHW030306100526

44590CB00012B/540